THE ART & CRAFT

OF THE

BLACKSMITH

TECHNIQUES AND INSPIRATION
FOR THE MODERN SMITH

T0383489

ROBERT THOMAS

Smithing can be a dangerous activity. Failure to follow safety procedures may result in serious injury or death. This book provides useful instruction, but we cannot anticipate all of your working conditions or the characteristics of your materials and tools. For your safety, you should use caution, care, and good judgment when following the procedures described in this book. Consider your own skill level and the instructions and safety precautions associated with the various tools and materials shown. The publisher cannot assume responsibility for any damage to property or injury to persons as a result of misuse of the information provided.

Brimming with creative inspiration, how-to projects, and useful information to enrich your everyday life, Quarto Knows is a favorite destination for those pursuing their interests and passions. Visit our site and dig deeper with our books into your area of interest: Quarto Creates, Quarto Cooks, Quarto Homes, Quarto Lives, Quarto Drives, Quarto Explores, Quarto Gifts, or Quarto Kids.

© 2018 Quarto Publishing Group USA Inc.
Text © 2018 Robert Thomas

First Published in 2018 by Quarry Books, an imprint of The Quarto Group, 100 Cummings Center, Suite 265-D, Beverly, MA 01915, USA.
T (978) 282-9590 F (978) 283-2742
QuartoKnows.com

All rights reserved. No part of this book may be reproduced in any form without written permission of the copyright owners. All images in this book have been reproduced with the knowledge and prior consent of the artists concerned, and no responsibility is accepted by producer, publisher, or printer for any infringement of copyright or otherwise, arising from the contents of this publication. Every effort has been made to ensure that credits accurately comply with information supplied. We apologize for any inaccuracies that may have occurred and will resolve inaccurate or missing information in a subsequent reprinting of the book.

Quarry Books titles are also available at discount for retail, wholesale, promotional, and bulk purchase. For details, contact the Special Sales Manager by email at specialsales@quarto.com or by mail at The Quarto Group, Attn: Special Sales Manager, 100 Cummings Center, Suite 265-D, Beverly, MA 01915, USA.

ISBN: 978-1-63159-381-9

Library of Congress Cataloging-in-Publication Data is available

Design: Paul Burgess at Burge Agency
Photography: Sully Sullivan Photography www.ohsully.com, except pages 5, 9, 28, 29, 34, 35, 47, 74, 75, 76, 80, 86, 87, 88, 89, 90, 91, 139, 145, courtesy of the craftsmen, and Shutterstock, pages 25, 26, 27

TO MY PARENTS, BOB AND ANGELA
THOMAS. MOM, THANK YOU FOR TEACHING
ME TO DRAW AND SEE THE WORLD LIKE AN
ARTIST. DAD, THANK YOU FOR TEACHING
ME TO WORK WITH MY HANDS AND THINK
LIKE AN ENGINEER.

CONTENTS

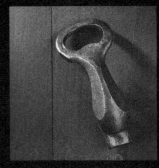

STEEL CAN TAKE ON NO OTHER FORM THAN ITS CURRENT ONE FOR THE PERSON WHO CANNOT WORK WITH IT. BUT ANY FORM IS ITS CURRENT ONE FOR THE MACHINIST OR BLACKSMITH.

Robert M. Pirsig, *Zen and the Art of Motorcycle Maintenance*

Meet the Robert Thomas Iron Design team: left to right: Tyler Bickerstaff, J. Powers Shepard, Matt Garton, and Robert Thomas.

PREFACE

ONE OF MY FAVORITE ASPECTS OF THE CRAFT OF BLACKSMITHING IS THE SENSE OF COMMUNITY THAT GROWS FROM INVOLVEMENT IN THE VARIOUS NATIONAL AND INTERNATIONAL BLACKSMITH ORGANIZATIONS. MANY OF THESE ORGANIZATIONS HOST LARGE FESTIVALS AND COMPETITIONS THROUGHOUT NORTH AMERICA AND EUROPE. IT IS AT THESE EVENTS THAT FRIENDSHIPS ARE BORN AND TECHNIQUES ARE SHARED THAT INEVITABLY LEAD TO INNOVATION WITHIN THE CRAFT. THEY ARE ALSO A GREAT PLACE TO PARTY.

One such festival, called Hefaiston, in the Czech Republic, hosts blacksmiths from around the world for an open forum, competition, and exhibition of the best work in the world. During my first trip to the festival, I ended up at a bar full of blacksmiths after a day of competitive forging listening to stories from forges around the world. After a lengthy discussion about the merits of a career in blacksmithing, a Swedish blacksmith leaned over the table and asked, "What's the difference between blacksmithing and heroin?"

Looking up from my giant glass of pilsner, I replied, "I don't know."

"You can quit heroin!" he said with a big grin on his face.

This was still relatively early in my journey as a blacksmith, but I knew he was right. I knew it the first time I ever struck a piece of hot steel years earlier. Pulling that first 2,000-degree bar out of the fire and watching it mold like modeling clay under the hammer, I knew I would never be able to quit.

Up until that point in my life, everything I had ever done, every job or career I tried my hand at, felt temporary, transitional—okay until I found something more exciting. Within an instant of forging my first piece of hot steel, I knew it was what I wanted to do for the rest of my life. I didn't quite understand how I would make it a career or what work I would produce—that would come later. I just knew I wanted to forge.

In talking to other smiths over the years, I've come to realize my experience was not unique. Many great smiths around the world were doing something else until they forged for the first time and then everything changed. Forging has a way of taking hold of you until it becomes part of who you are.

Blacksmiths have been forging metal for thousands of years, and we still haven't done it all. For me, that knowledge makes the craft especially inspiring. I know I will never totally master this craft because it can never be totally mastered. As soon as I pursue all I can in one direction, I'll realize there is more to pursue somewhere else. This means it can never get dull; it can never get monotonous. There will always be some aesthetic to chase, some technique to

perfect, and something to strive for. I will always be a student of the craft.

My career is not about attaining mastery—it's about pursuing it.

Within weeks of that first forging session, I was on a plane flying to England for my interview at Hereford College of Arts for their Artistic Blacksmithing degree program. During my time in Hereford, I learned how to work with the anvil and the sketchbook to develop an aesthetic style. After school, working in commercial shops, I learned how to translate that style into production ironwork.

My journey as a blacksmith has always been exciting and allowed me to meet and work with incredible blacksmiths from all over the world. Along the way, I've even been able to convince some of them to come work with me. I've been very fortunate, and now I have a very well equipped forging studio and a great team of blacksmiths to work with everyday. My work is an ever evolving expression of who I am as an artist, but it is the Robert Thomas Iron Design (RTID) team that makes the expression possible. I really don't even think of myself as a singular artist very much anymore since almost everything I create is a collaboration with the RTID team: Tyler Bickerstaff, Matt Garton, J. Powers Shepard, and myself. Power hammers and hydraulic presses are great, but no tool can replace the support and enthusiasm of a fellow blacksmith.

I am often asked if it's still as exciting as it used to be—working with the fire and swinging a hammer and getting dirty. The short answer is yes. No matter what else I have going on in my day, from client meetings to design work, when I finally get on that fire and watch the material squish and deform and stretch, it's as if there is nothing else—only me, the fire, and the steel. It's like being a kid playing in a sandbox.

People also ask, "Isn't it hard work?" Yes.

"Isn't it hot?" Yes.

"Don't you get burned?" Yes.

"Aren't there easier ways to make a living?" Definitely yes!

They rarely ask, "Why do you do it?" Instead they say something like, "That must be the coolest job ever! I wish I could do that."

To which I say: You can. A blacksmith can come from anywhere and start with any background. All you have to do is pick up the hammer and put in the hours.

INTENT

What I seek to achieve in writing this book is to offer a primer for craftspeople who may have had a taste of basic blacksmithing techniques and are now hoping to bring their practice to the next level. We'll look at iron as a tool and medium and dig into some of the subject matter that you'll need to know to gain a deeper understanding of your craft. And lastly, we'll go through some basic, intermediate, and advanced techniques and then work through projects specifically designed to use those skills.

The goal of this book is to present the blacksmith's craft within a modern, professional context: to present blacksmithing in such a way that provides the reader with the perspective on how to contribute to the world of current design using blacksmithing techniques to create large and small pieces of functional art that stand on design as well as craftsmanship.

Here is a monumental staircase railing we forged for a commercial project. The architect came to us with an aesthetic idea, and we worked together to design as much forging into the project as possible. The project consists of four flights and multiple complex transitions.

PART I:
IRON

Forging transforms the shape of hot steel using localized compressive forces—in this case, the dies of our 100 kg Beche power hammer.

WHAT IS METAL?

Two bars lie prepped and ready to be fire welded—the process by which all iron and steel bars were fused before the advent of electric welding.

PEOPLE REALIZED THAT PLACING NATURALLY-OCCURRING COPPER IN THE KILNS USED TO FIRE POTTERY WOULD CAUSE IT TO SOFTEN AND ALLOW IT TO BE WORKED WITH HAMMERS AND CHISELS. IT CANNOT BE OVERSTATED HOW REVOLUTIONARY THIS WAS.

Humans had culture. They could develop common values, identity, and purpose. They formed the tight bonds of family and the looser bonds of community and state. They codified those bonds with symbols and ceremonies, foods and holidays, and churches and civic institutions. They made peace, or war, with outsiders. These qualities and others allowed generations of thinkers to set the human animal above all others. But today, nearly every one of the characteristics those early thinkers assumed set man above beast has been discovered in animal species.

Scientists studying dolphins in Russia have found evidence they use both grammar and syntax—key components in advanced language. Chimpanzees and bonobos in Africa not only use tools, but teach tool use to their children. Bower birds decorate their homes. Ants and bees make war. So what is our claim to a unique legacy?

I say metal.

METAL MAKES US HUMAN.

When we knew little about the world around us, telling the difference between humans and animals was easy. There were physical distinctions: humans stood upright, walked on two legs.

Humans had language. They could feel and give voice to complex emotions, sharing with each other a rich inner life.

Humans had artifice. They could make tools tailored to specific tasks and refine those tools over time. They could decorate their environment to be pleasing to the eye.

THE BEGINNING OF IRON

Humans have existed for hundreds of thousands of years, and for much of that time, we were a uniquely intelligent and successful species of animals. We made simple tools and cooperated to hunt and gather food. We decorated the walls of caves with drawings. We assume we sang songs and told stories, but this will probably never be proven.

That changed beginning around 7,500 years ago, with the Chalcolithic, or Copper Age. In various places around the world—the mountains of Serbia, the Fertile Crescent in Iraq, Anatolia in Turkey, and others—people realized that placing naturally-occurring copper in the kilns used to fire pottery would cause it to soften and allow it to be worked with hammers and chisels.

It cannot be overstated how revolutionary this was. Copper was a beautiful and ductile metal, flowing smoothly into wire of almost impossible fineness or sheets as thin as paper. A copper mace head would not shatter like stone. A copper jug would not break like pottery. Most important of all, items made of copper did not degrade over time. They were ideal instruments of trade, able to be kept in times of plenty and bartered when other things were needed.

People who could work and shape copper became the first specialist craftspeople in human history— the first smiths.

Transporting copper goods may have spurred early efforts to domesticate horses, and copper cladding for early plows sped the growth of agriculture. Economy, commerce, stable

Copper can be forged, but with a different temperature range than steel. Most forms that can be formed in steel can also be forged from copper.

communities, and farm animals, all grew from one skill, the ability to work copper.

But as an industrial material, copper is limited; it is too ductile to hold its shape under stress and is not hard enough to hold a sharp edge for long. The realization, about 6,000 years ago, that combining copper with arsenic or tin resulted in an entirely new metal— bronze—rewrote civilization again. Bronze was the first metal hard enough to be made into swords and armor: tools of war that had no analogues in prehistory.

Many of the societies of antiquity we admire, like the Greeks, ascended because of their mastery of bronze. In the wake of their conquests, they built trading networks and mutual protection pacts that necessitated new forms of governance—democracy and empire.

To glue these polities together, culture blossomed, with art forms and stories that are still enjoyed today—like that of Prometheus, a metaphor for the smith, who stole from the gods the fire of creation.

Miners in Britain, Turkmenistan, and central Europe, seeking copper and tin for bronze production, were some of the first people to bring iron ore to the surface. As bronze was a qualitative improvement over copper, so iron was over bronze. It was more plentiful than bronze. Not every village had bronze, but every village had iron. The final ingredient in human civilization—writing—came at the beginning of the Iron Age. Writing allowed the complex techniques and skills of working with iron (and later, steel) to be preserved and disseminated.

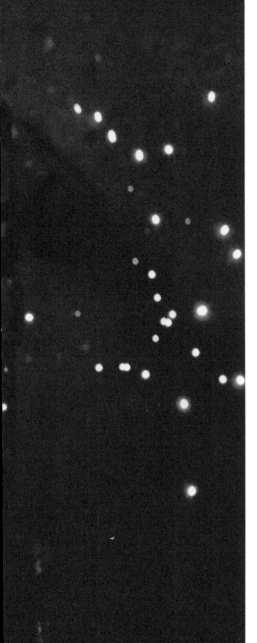

TYPES OF IRON

DIFFERENT TERMS FOR IRON ARE USED IN THIS BOOK: WROUGHT IRON, CAST IRON, AND STEEL. THE DIFFERENCES BETWEEN THESE TYPES OF IRON LIE IN THE WAY THEY ARE CREATED AND WORKED, THEIR CHEMICAL COMPOSITION, AND THEIR PHYSICAL PROPERTIES.

Iron begins in the bodies of stars. Stellar fusion, the method by which stars create their heat and light, collides atoms together with such speed and force that new configurations of subatomic particles are formed. Hydrogen, the lightest and simplest of elements, is present in all stars. But as stars become larger and more dense, heavier elements are formed by fusion. Helium is the next heaviest. Then there's lithium, the lightest metal, and so on.

But there is an upper limit to the size and lifespan of stars. Some stars grow so large that their immense gravity causes an explosion, called a supernova, that expels most of their matter throughout the blackness of space for light-years in every direction. In such enormous, dense, unstable stars, iron is the last element created by their fusion before they explode.

Iron is the most common metal in the universe. It forms most of the mass of rocky planets like Earth—for all the iron structures we see on the surface of the Earth, most of our iron is inside our planet's core. It is the twenty-sixth heaviest element: one of the transition metals on the periodic table. Transition metals have metallic properties and open spaces in their outer electron shells, making them attractive for other atoms to attach.

This structure allows iron atoms to hook together in tight patterns, giving iron its durability and strength. Iron atoms also pair easily with oxygen atoms, causing a number of chemical side-effects, from the rusting on the outside of an iron beam to the iron-rich hemoglobin carrying oxygen in your blood.

A high-carbon tool steel forging. The higher carbon content gives the tool superior strength and toughness as compared to wrought iron.

PIG IRON, WROUGHT IRON, CAST IRON, AND STEEL

Outside of a laboratory, it's very rare to find completely pure iron. Smelting, the process of extracting iron from ore, causes the iron atoms to bond with a small amount of the carbon from fire and smoke. This addition of carbon is what allowed iron to claim its place in human history.

Without carbon, iron is brittle—pure iron can actually crumble into powder. With the addition of carbon, oxygen, and occasionally other metals, however, the iron can be strengthened into workable forms. But there is a small window. Too many impurities and the iron goes right back to being brittle. The sweet spot is narrow—a piece of iron whose carbon and impurities make up more than five or six percent of its weight is nearly useless.

Early iron was known as pig iron, so called because it was made by pouring molten iron into little molds that looked like a sow with suckling piglets. It dates back over 4,000 years and usually has a high carbon content.

To refine pig iron into something useful, it must be worked. Using heat, air currents, and brute force, impurities and carbon are removed from the metal. The percentage of remaining carbon determines the type of metal you have.

Iron that is extremely pure—less than a tenth of a percent by weight in carbon—is wrought iron. If the weight of impurities is greater than two percent, the metal is known as cast iron. And iron in the middle of these two extremes is steel, which is more durable than its predecessors: wrought and cast.

Though steel existed in antiquity, it was not viable on an industrial scale until Englishman Henry Bessemer patented the Bessemer Process in 1856. As the first method of removing impurities from massive quantities of pig iron at once, the Bessemer Process drove the price of steel down and increased the supply. The more labor-intensive methods required by wrought iron drove it out of favor. Mild steel production overtook wrought iron in the 1920s. Today, only steel and cast iron are still in production.

Almost all contemporary blacksmithing is done using steel. Wrought iron is not produced anywhere in the world anymore save for a few places that recycle it, and it is usually only used in historical reproduction work that specifically calls for it. So, when we say wrought iron today, we are really referring to a type of ironwork rather than a specific material: specifically, iron that has been hammered and worked by hand.

WHAT IS FORGING?

A decorative element is forged down to a drastic point using localized compressive forces from a radiused die on the power hammer.

The same element is forged using localized compressive forces from hand hammer and anvil.

There are several ways to make a desired part from steel. Most processes boil down to three basic methods: forging, machining, and casting. A desired shape can be machined out of a larger chunk by removing excess stock with mechanical means. This can be done using machines like mills and lathes or by hand using grinders and files. A shape can also be cast by pouring molten metal into a mold of the part. The same shape is forged by molding the steel into a different shape than it started as.

Forging refers to the forming of metal by compression. It is the oldest way of working metal known to man. Before man had the technology to machine or cast, there were blacksmiths hammering on hot iron. A piece is forged when it is deformed to the point that it's cross-sectional dimension is changed. At a molecular level, the grain structure of the material is compacted and directed during the forging process, adding strength with every blow of the hammer. At the same time, porosity is eliminated.

In industry, forging is a process known to make the strongest, most durable parts. Parts are created by forging, casting, and machining for different purposes, but the hardest working parts are generally forged. Whether it's a lawnmower engine or nuclear submarine, if it needs to be as strong as possible, it's forged.

Over the last millennium, the word forged has become synonymous with strength in literal and metaphorical contexts. For the purposes of decorative and sculptural forgework, the added strength gained during the forging process is usually redundant. The feelings and connotations conjured up by the knowledge that something is forged become a design statement.

FORGING VS. FABRICATION

Fabrication is the process of cutting, bending, and assembling metal parts to create finished products. The connection method for the assembly process is usually, but not always, electric welding. Most blacksmiths are also fabricators, but most fabricators are not blacksmiths. Any blacksmith who assembles work with multiple components is also a fabricator, although they will usually be quick to correct you if you call them a fabricator.

Within the context of architectural ironwork, the distinction between the craftsperson who identifies as a blacksmith and the one who identifies as a fabricator lies in the sourcing of their parts. Fabricators avoid forgework and often assemble prefabricated components or forgings purchased from vendors. Blacksmiths forge their own. The use of prefabricated components has time and cost savings, but in the forging of your own lies the opportunity to innovate and push the limits of the material.

Joining two bars with a riveted connection is technically fabrication, but the hammering over of the hot rivet head is blacksmithing. All blacksmiths are fabricators, but not all fabricators are blacksmiths.

Tyler forges a custom strap hinge for a historic restoration project. Products like this are now almost exclusively mass-produced overseas to a low standard of quality. Educating the customer on the hand-forging process helps them understand the value of hiring a local blacksmith instead.

THE ROLE OF THE SMITH

FOR MUCH OF HISTORY, THE MOST EDUCATED PERSON YOU WERE LIKELY TO MEET WAS A SMITH. HE OR SHE WAS MORE LIKELY THAN THEIR NEIGHBORS TO BE LITERATE, AND THEIR TRADE WAS THE END PRODUCT OF A LENGTHY AND FORMAL TRAINING PERIOD.

A smith's forge was the center of many small communities. Smiths could travel, own property, perform marriages, and amass fortunes. They had economic and class mobility of a kind that would not be widely available until the modern era. And most crucially, they were innovative. Smiths could recycle metal, refine designs, change chemical compositions, and invent wholly new devices.

The technological age we inhabit today seems very far from our metalworking heritage—we have a Silicon Valley, our cars are made of fiberglass, and we use so much plastic we now have a plastic island in the middle of the Pacific Ocean. But the chips and batteries in the phone in your pocket are made with so-called rare earths—metals, like neodymium and gadolinium, whose secrets are still being unlocked and whose extraction and processing are extremely controversial. Similar chips could one day control nanobots that will revolutionize medicine. And the physical sciences originally developed to understand the properties of metal are today used in the field of astrophysics, as scientists analyze heavenly bodies to answer the most fundamental questions of the universe.

The study of metal is still crucial for our future, even if it now takes place largely in labs and not the smithy in the center of town. But there have been tradeoffs. We no longer see the effort that goes into our possessions and are too cavalier with the responsibility to maintain them. Purchase decisions are design and cost driven with little regard for durability or longevity. The modern blacksmith is competing with sweatshop laborers half a world away. Educating the consumer on the differences between the hand-forging and mass-production is an essential part of the sales process.

It is too much to say that returning to artisan metalwork is enough to cure all society's ills. But recognizing the centrality of metal to the human experience means recognizing fundamental truths about ourselves—our innovation, creativity, resourcefulness, artistry, and power. Live too long away from those attributes and the result is stagnation and pessimism.

We live in the early years of a century which could see an end to cancer and hunger, which could put people on Mars, and develop sources of unlimited clean energy. But many Americans believe our best days are behind us— perhaps because they have never had the opportunity of staring at a piece of cold iron and knowing that with the right application of heat and ingenuity it could become a unique railing element or beautiful screen for the front of a fireplace. In looking forward at the challenges of the coming century, the forge—and the blacksmith—still have much to teach.

THE HISTORY OF DECORATIVE IRON

IN 1517, MARTIN LUTHER DROVE AN IRON NAIL THROUGH HIS *NINETY-FIVE THESES* AND INTO THE DOOR OF THE CATHEDRAL IN WITTENBERG, GERMANY, OPENING UP A NEW CHAPTER IN EUROPEAN HISTORY. UP UNTIL THAT POINT, THE CONTINENT'S DOMINANT POLITICAL INSTITUTION WAS THE ROMAN CATHOLIC CHURCH, WHICH HAD WITHSTOOD CRITICISM AND HERESY FOR OVER A THOUSAND YEARS. WITH THE PROTESTANT REFORMATION, HOWEVER, FOR THE FIRST TIME, THE POWER OF THE CHURCH AND THE MANY CATHOLIC MONARCHIES IT SUPPORTED WAS UNDER SERIOUS THREAT.

BAROQUE AND ROCOCO

At around the same time, innovations in technology were changing the process of making and using iron. Higher quality iron was being produced at lower prices, making it more accessible. And changes in warfare were rendering armored knights obsolete, freeing up iron for other purposes.

Taken together, these social and technological trends meant that the largest political body in the western world—the Catholic Church—needed to make a show of splendor, might, and perpetual power just as one of the strongest metals was dropping in price and becoming easier to make.

The result was the Baroque period, one of the earliest Western aesthetic movements to make extensive use of decorative iron. The intent of Baroque design was to be visually overwhelming—a reminder of the Church and monarchy's divinely-granted authority. Baroque design features complex curves, strong lines, symmetry, and grandeur. Baroque architecture is still associated with power—your local bank might have a Baroque column or two flanking the door to its vault.

Iron in Baroque design was both intricate and monumental. Throughout Europe, iron replaced wood in rood screens—physical barriers designed to separate the clergy in cathedrals. To attend Mass meant to witness the miracle of transubstantiation through arabesques and curls of iron.

Eventually, the Baroque style overtook most of Europe and Protestant England. Some of the most beautiful Baroque ironwork to survive to this day is at Hampton Court Palace in England. Crafted by the French master Jean Tijou, the elaborately gilded gates and screens represent the nations in the United Kingdom, showing the English crown's dominance over all its subjects.

Here's an iconic example of Baroque ironwork: Gates and screens by French master Jean Tijou commissioned by William and Mary for Hampton Court Palace.

The Baroque masterpieces at Hampton Court, however, heralded the transition to come. Hampton Court Palace was originally built by one of the last Catholic advisors to an English monarch—Cardinal Wolsey, who was charged with treason by his sovereign Henry VIII. During Henry's reign, England became one of the most powerful Protestant nations in the world, stamping its permanence and authority using the decorative grammar of the Catholic continent. Over 100 years later, the iconic ironwork of Hampton Court Palace would be commissioned by Protestant co-regents William and Mary.

Hampton Court shows how the cultural tides that Baroque design attempted to stem could not be controlled. A new world order emerged from the Protestant Reformation, one with strong Catholic and Protestant kingdoms whose destinies were intertwined and whose power grew as colonialism and trade spread across the world. A new decorative movement sprang from this new order, one which abandoned rigid symmetry and stiff grandeur.

The Rococo period was lighter and more whimsical. The heavy colors and formality of the Baroque period gave way to pastels and curlicues—innovations made possible by new textiles, dyes, and enamels from far-flung colonies and trading partners, as well as further advances at the forge.

To this day, Rococo design suggests lightness, femininity, and innocence, whether it's seen in a little girl's tea set or a sparkling chandelier. But that innocence was doomed. The blithe monarchies who frolicked through the Rococo period's candy-colored excesses were in for a seismic upheaval to their way of life.

REVOLUTIONS

The revolutions in America and France were contemporaneous with another, slower revolution in England. In 1783, an ironmaster named Henry Cort patented the first puddling furnace, a system where iron was melted without ever touching the fuel. Within a few decades, Cort's method had changed the entire economy of northern England, planting the seeds for the Industrial Revolution of the nineteenth century.

Gone from fashion was the excess of Baroque and Rococo design. The new world, founded on the democratic principles of the austere Athenians and the ruthless forces of the market, called for a new period of design—the Neoclassical, much simpler in ornament. Iron, now available in unprecedented quantity and purity, began to assume a structural role in the construction of factories, warehouses, and mills.

Of course, there is no more famous example of the structural possibilities of wrought iron than that which was erected on the Champ de Mars by Gustave Eiffel in 1887. The Eiffel Tower was so radical a departure from the old-fashioned beauty of Paris that hundreds of artists and thinkers protested its construction, saying it would be "a gigantic black smokestack" and "a hateful column of bolted sheet metal." Today, when the Eiffel Tower is one of the most beloved and recognizable monuments in the world, the criticism might make you smile. But, it was a foreshadowing of the backlash that was to come against modern and industrial design.

This is a low-angle shot of the Eiffel tower in Paris. It was assembled using 2.5 million rivets to hold together 7,300 tons (6,600,000 kg) of wrought iron.

Designed by Hector Guimard, the Abbesses metro station in Paris is a great example of Art Nouveau Ironwork.

COUNTERREVOLUTIONS

The late nineteenth and early twentieth centuries saw a flowering of alternative design movements to counter the stark and utilitarian look of the industrialized world—and iron played an important role in all of them. The Beaux-Arts style reached all the way back to the Baroque period for its rich and eclectic ornamentation, which included intricate ironwork.

In England, the Arts and Crafts Exhibition Society held its first show in 1887, coincidentally the same year as the debut of the Eiffel Tower. The Society sought to return to traditional methods and aesthetics, including hand-wrought iron, bringing back the high standards associated with master craftsmen in the era before mass production. Arts and Crafts design favored simple, high-quality materials and restrained ornamentation drawn from nature. It had a huge influence on the later style of Art Nouveau: the pinnacle of wrought iron's grace, complexity, and beauty.

Art Nouveau wrought iron designers like Victor Horta, Hector Guimard, and Louis Comfort Tiffany favored lush, organic forms, radical asymmetry, and breaking the two-dimensional plane. The result is a romantic and dramatic aesthetic that is still beloved today, whether it's seen in the unique stations of the Paris metro or a Tiffany lamp casting a warm glow over many a modern living room.

DECLINE AND RENAISSANCE

The premium placed on high quality materials and craftsmanship by the Arts and Crafts and Art Nouveau movements was no match for the commercial logic of mass production. Cast iron, and later, steel, both dropped in price steadily during the twentieth century, making them more economical and popular choices for ornamental metalwork. Advances in glass and concrete production allowed for innovations in design that had little use for the hand-crafted and increasingly old-fashioned aesthetic of wrought iron. Bauhaus and Brutalism styles formed the template for rebuilding a broken Europe after World War II, and in the U.S., glass-sheathed skyscrapers forever rewrote the book on monumental architecture.

The last wrought iron foundry in the world closed in 1973. Today, all wrought iron is produced by recycling, and many wrought iron craftspeople, including myself, work with steel. But the social and cultural forces—the hunger for permanence and grandeur, the desire for handmade and high-quality craftsmanship, and the inherent fascination of working lifeless metal into living, beautiful forms—that propelled the rise of wrought iron in the last millennium are still with us now, in the early years of the new one.

They find expression in innovative buildings that are returning to metal as design statement, like the Beijing National Stadium—subject to some of the same kinds of criticism as the Eiffel Tower was in its day. And they find expression in the improbable flourishing of modern blacksmithing, as people all over the world return to the forge. These craftspeople are the beneficiaries of a thousand years of design elements—Baroque and Rococo, Neoclassical and Art Nouveau—all preserved by the endurance of iron as a medium. In remixing and innovating from the idioms of the past, blacksmiths today are making a new and vibrant art form for the future.

This is an ornamental gate and fence project we completed in Pittsburgh. This project involved designing and forging a new arch and gates, as well as restoring and integrating antique wrought and cast iron fencing. The design called for the mixing of several architectural styles and the construction called for mixing of several new and antique material types.

PART II:
TECHNIQUE AND TOOLING

THE HAND-FORGED AESTHETIC

This forged chandelier has elements that are obviously handmade but still clean and precise. Multiple surface textures make the elements stand out and help the viewer differentiate it from something mass-produced. All pieces are held together with tension and can easily be released by pulling the central pin.

THE GOAL OF THE PROJECTS IN THIS BOOK IS TO CREATE PIECES OF FUNCTIONAL ART, FULFILLING BOTH THE ARTISTIC AND PRACTICAL POTENTIAL OF THE CRAFT OF BLACKSMITHING. THROUGHOUT MUCH OF HISTORY, THE BLACKSMITH'S ROLE WAS UTILITARIAN AS WELL AS ARTISTIC. BLACKSMITHS MADE MANY FUNCTIONAL OBJECTS, SO THE GOAL IN DECORATIVE WORK OFTEN WAS TO NOT HIGHLIGHT THE FORGING PROCESS. PIECES WERE REFINED AND WORKED MORE SO THAN THEY ARE TODAY. IN HISTORICAL REPRODUCTION BLACKSMITHING, THIS IS STILL THE STYLE PRIZED FOR ITS AUTHENTICITY.

The buying habits of today's consumer, however, are driven by design, rather than durability. Fashion changes quickly, so many mass-produced decorative items, including pieces of ironwork, are churned out quickly and using low-quality materials and processes.

To differentiate themselves in a mass-produced market, modern blacksmiths create work that does NOT look like it was mass-produced; they seek a hand-forged aesthetic. If a blacksmith creates a piece that is no different than something that can be mass-produced, the consumer doesn't benefit in any way from the additional time and expense of the hand-forged process. For some consumers, simply supporting a craftsperson is reason enough for a purchase, but I think they should be able to have something that has superior craftsmanship and design.

The hand-forged aesthetic gives the consumer artistic features they would not have if the piece was mass-produced, making it worthwhile to spend a little extra. Simply put, it gives them value.

FORGED ARTISTRY

The other side of the hand-forged aesthetic is artistry. I don't necessarily mean that all pieces of smithing need to be sculptural or something that would appear in a gallery. But the visible difference imparted on objects by exceptional craft—precise joinery, beautifully tapered bars, intricate scrollwork, and elegant terminations—provides ample opportunity for artistry.

An example of what I mean can be found in the mortise and tenon joint. This is a form of joinery that has been around for millennia and offers incredible strength. It is also a challenging joint for the blacksmith and opportunity to show off some skill. You might be tempted to downplay this joint and hide its structural qualities in your work—but why? It takes a lot longer to

create compared to a welded joint. If, however, you highlight this joint as a design feature by leaving the drifted hole swollen out and making the hammered tenon prominent, then the joint becomes an integral part of the design. The highlighted joint becomes part of the story of a piece, while the hidden joint shortens that story.

Here is a driveway and pedestrian gate project we completed in downtown Charleston. Multiple bars come together using mortise-and-tenon joinery. The swelled holes and hammered tenons turn what would have been boring intersections into design elements.

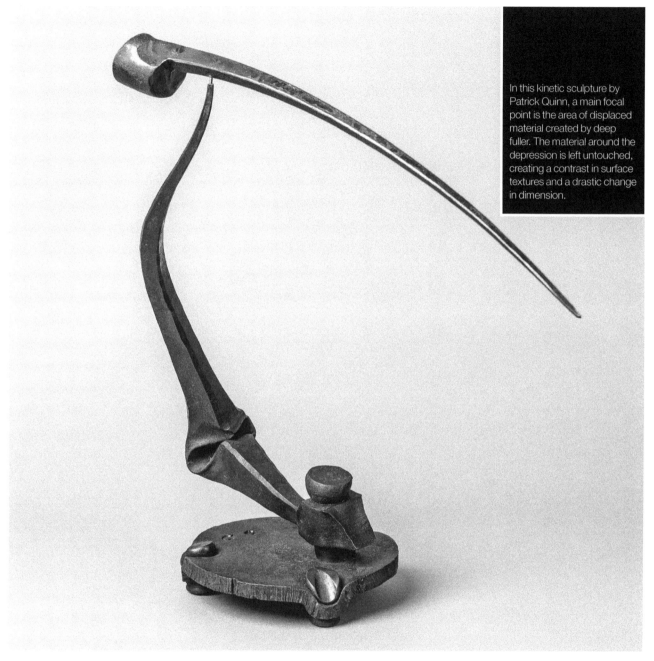

In this kinetic sculpture by Patrick Quinn, a main focal point is the area of displaced material created by deep fuller. The material around the depression is left untouched, creating a contrast in surface textures and a drastic change in dimension.

The contemporary blacksmith may use the same tools as the historical smith, but in a slightly different way to achieve different results. Traditional blacksmith tooling, like swages, fullers, punches, and set hammers, were designed for specific purposes to make specific products hundreds of years ago. Now, many of these products are made by machines and no longer need to be made by these tools. The modern smith often uses these same tools to create different forms than they were originally designed to create. They might spread out material and then leave it spread instead of tucking the corners back in and squaring it up like a traditional blacksmith would have done in the nineteenth century. Sometimes, it is the area not touched by the hammer, but deformed indirectly, that produces the desired aesthetic. Today, a blacksmith may create a stylized furniture component with a tool that was designed to make plough shears.

Future blacksmith extraordinaire Rhett Thomas can tell you that safety gear is just as important for shop visitors as it is for blacksmiths. Her monkey socks are actually steel-toed.

SAFETY

At the beginning of any craft book, the first thing that needs to be discussed is safety, and this one is no different. The modern blacksmith workshop can seem like a very dangerous place and it often is, but with proper safety precautions the risk is minimized. Basic personal safety is a matter of remembering eyes, ears, and toes. Safety glasses, ear protection, and protective boots are an absolute must. Other things like leather aprons, gloves, and protective sleeves are used when appropriate depending on personal preference.

Workshop safety best practices can go a long way toward making the forge a safe working environment. The forging area should be kept clean and organized with tools not left on the floor in traffic areas. In the midst of a project, this can be a difficult but important task.

Working as a blacksmith, one gets used to being around fire and sparks very quickly. At first, it can seem like you have to stand ten feet away from the fire to avoid singed skin. After a short time, you'll realize that fire is a tool that should be respected, but used to its maximum potential. When controlled properly, there is nothing to be afraid of. Every blacksmith gets burned. It will happen often at first and with less frequency as you gain proficiency. Small burns should be treated immediately by running the burn (usually on your hand or arm) under cold water. For more severe burns, you may need to seek medical attention.

The use of gloves while doing small hand forged work is often debated. I believe that gloves should only be worn when they absolutely need to be, and you should never wear a glove on your hammer hand. The only exception is when you're hammering a piece that's throwing off so much heat that it burns your knuckles on your hammer hand. You surrender a lot of control with the use of gloves, and that control often does more to prevent burns than the glove would. For instance, when holding a heated bar on the cold end, you'll be able to tell how far down the bar in the direction of the heat you can grab very easily with a bare hand. In the time you're

forging, the heat is not likely to transfer up the bar to the point that you can't grab it. Conversely, if you grab the bar with a gloved hand, it may seem cool enough when you grab it, but the heat will come through the glove while you're forging and you'll be forced to readjust your grip, throwing off your workflow.

THE WORKSHOP

THE BLACKSMITH'S WORKSHOP GOES BY SEVERAL DIFFERENT NAMES: FORGE, SMITHY, STUDIO, SHOP. WHATEVER YOU CALL IT, THE WORKSHOP CAN BE A 10 FOOT BY 10 FOOT (3 × 3 M) SHED OR A 100,000 SQUARE FOOT (9,290 M²) BUILDING AND ANYTHING IN BETWEEN. THE ONLY QUALIFICATION IS THAT IT'S YOUR PLACE TO FORGE STEEL.

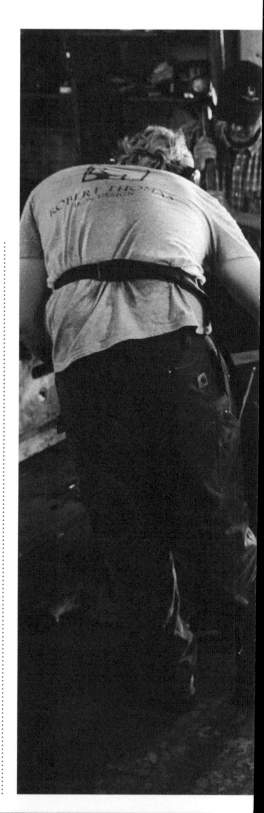

Workshops tend to take on different shapes and layouts depending on the work moving through them. If your work is primarily small items like housewares or small-scale sculpture, you may only need a small room with a fire, an anvil, and a few other select tools. If you want to take on more sizeable architectural commissions, it can be helpful, but not required, to have a larger space. The size of your space will also be dependent on how many people you intend to work with. If you intend to work alone, a large space can be a lot of work just to keep up with cleaning and maintenance. When I worked alone, I preferred to have a smaller space (about 800 square feet [74 m²]). Now that there are 4 to 5 of us working in the shop at the same time, it's great to have 5000 square feet (465 m²) to move around in.

In my travels, I get to see some really unique workshops, and each and every one has something about it that is special and ingenious. I still take every opportunity I can to see other smith's workshops. It seems like every time I do, I notice a great idea for improving my own workshop. Many smiths spend their entire career refining the systems and environment in which they work and are happy to show off their spaces to interested craftspeople.

The Japanese have a manufacturing philosophy called *kaizen*, which means to improve. It applies to everyone and every aspect of a manufacturing organization—from the CEO to the janitor and from the most expensive piece of machinery down to the mailbox. In its essence, it means to always strive to do something better than you did the last time. In the world of the blacksmith, this can mean to constantly improve your workflow. A huge contributor to workflow efficiency is workshop setup. Even if profit is not your goal, it still feels good to know you're doing things efficiently and effectively. Take the time to set your workspace up carefully and be prepared to keep refining it and improving it. Constantly walking around the shop looking for tools can be very frustrating. Having the tools where and when you need them gives you the freedom to concentrate on your creative process.

Tyler and Matt work Smith and Striker on the anvil while John Winer draws out a bar on the power hammer, and I refine a curve using the vise. Even larger workshops can get a little cramped when four people are working in the same area, but when everyone is working in harmony, the energy is great.

BASIC TOOLS

There are many different configurations for a blacksmith shop, and smiths will tell you that you need few tools to call yourself a blacksmith. That is true. Nonetheless, even the most historically accurate and minimalist shops will have an anvil, a forge, a slack tub, a post vise, hand tools, and most likely at least one power hammer or press.

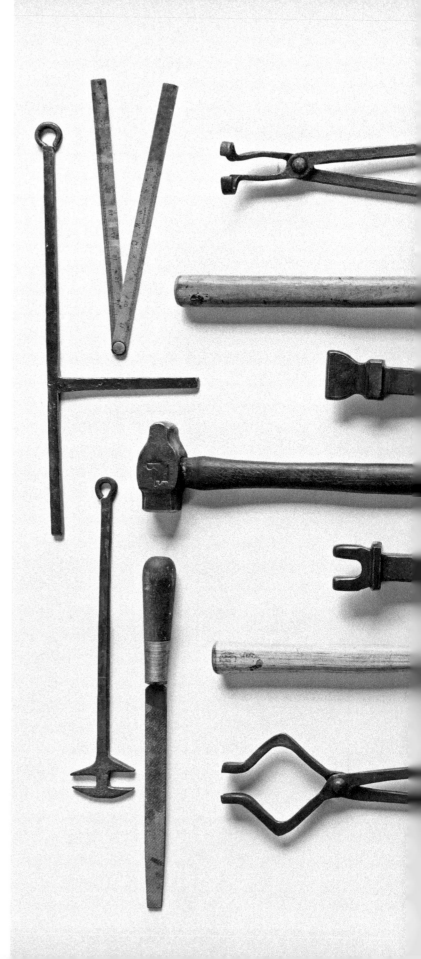

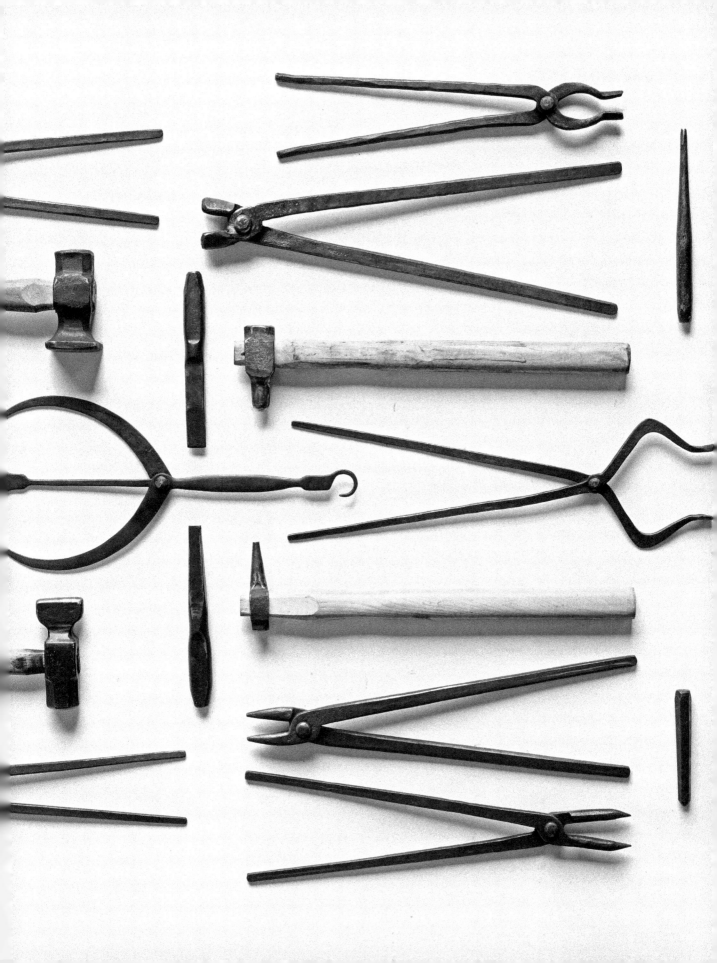

THE ANVIL

If I could describe blacksmithing as any one thing, it is the process of controlling kinetic energy to deform metal. A great deal of that energy comes from the anvil. This may sound counterintuitive; after all, an anvil is (one hopes) the most solid object in a smithy. It's still a cultural shorthand for massiveness, weight, and stability; long after most children are likely to encounter a blacksmith in real life, they still know what it means when an anvil is dropped on a cartoon character's head.

But when a blacksmith swings his or her hammer, they are expending kinetic energy, of which they have a limited supply. Smithing is hard work. To be able to work long hours crafting a fine piece of metal, the smith needs to be able to recoup as much of the energy they expend swinging their hammer as possible.

That's where the anvil comes in. An anvil is heavy enough to not shift when the blacksmith strikes it and hard enough to deflect the strength of the blow back up, returning a portion of the blacksmith's energy for the next swing. It's like running on asphalt: runners find it much easier than softer surfaces like sand.

To control the upswing and effectively use the returned energy, the shape of the anvil is important. Every curve, point, corner, and edge on the anvil has a specific function, and where the smith places the metal on the anvil allows for the creation of different effects.

On most anvils, those parts include a horn, or pointed conical section, used for shaping curve or thinning out metal (also called drawing down). It is the horn that gives the anvil its characteristic shape. Across from the horn, on the other side of the anvil, is the face, or work surface. Often, holes will be incised into the face to aid with punching and tooling; in fact, one of the holes, called a Hardy hole, has an entire set of tools specially crafted to slot into it and hold steady. Between the face and horn is usually a step, where chisels can be safely used. Of course, not every anvil conforms to this pattern; some anvils are used for specialist operations and have different shapes.

The main anvil in our shop dates from 1882 and was probably cast in England to create chains for tall ships. I like to think of the hundreds of years of history and countless swings of the hammer it has seen when we use it.

And use it we do; power hammers and hydraulic presses do not replace hammer and anvil in the modern blacksmith shop. We still use the anvil for shaping, finishing work, and occasionally, a technique called Smith and Striker.

Smith and Striker is a method of cooperation between two workers; in the days before power hammers, it was the only way to accomplish the backbreaking work of flattening bar iron. The smith is the more experienced; they hammer the metal in precisely the place they wish the striker to use more force, often with a much larger hammer. As smith guides and striker strikes, a rhythm is established.

Sometimes, we still use Smith and Striker, even though we have perfectly good power hammers just a few feet from the anvil. It's fun. And it's a fantastic reminder of the roots of our craft and a way to increase our connection as artists.

POWER HAMMERS

In our shop, we have three power hammers, spanning more than sixty years. You can use our power hammers to trace some pretty fascinating industrial trends.

The oldest and the smallest is our Little Giant hammer. Little Giant is an American manufacturer dating from 1895, the so-called Gilded Age.

America's Gilded Age fortunes were built on steel, oil, and railroads—the bones, blood, and circulatory system of the industrial revolution. When the Little Giant company first shipped its hammers, the largest steam power hammer in world history was churning out plate armor for battleships in Bethlehem, Pennsylvania— and terrifying the locals who thought the sound would cause earthquakes.

The scale and technology of Little Giant hammers was more modest. Most that were shipped had ram weights of 25 to 100 pounds (11 to 45 kg), and rather than being powered with steam, they were powered mechanically, with flywheels and centrifugal clutches.

When our Little Giant was built in 1953, America was experiencing a second industrial revolution, this one powered by consumer goods like automobiles and home appliances. It was the postwar economic boom, and America's manufacturing sector was uniquely poised to drive the global recovery.

Although it's nice to think that this hammer had a glamorous life forging iconic pieces of Americana, it likely spent 40 years putting points on jackhammer bits before being retired to the barn in rural South Carolina where I found it. Whatever its purpose, it and millions of hammers like it were the workhorses of the American economy for the crucial years following World War II.

Fast forward ten years, to 1963. Finally recovered from its war wounds, Germany was ramping up its own manufacturing sector. And in Germany, the hammer of choice was the Beche air hammer.

This is our 100 kg Beche L3 air hammer. Circa 1963.

Our Beche is the L3 100 kg model, and it's my pride and joy. The thing that is so amazing about it is the stunning standard of its engineering. When I bought this hammer, it had been in continuous service for over fifty years and looked brand new.

The Beche set such a standard for power hammer construction that its patent became a spoil of war. After the partitioning of Germany following World War II, the Soviet Union acquired the blueprints to the Beche and spread similar machines throughout the country and its allies' manufacturing sectors. That included China, which built and still builds the Anyang power hammer to a very similar design to this day.

The third hammer I have is a 40 kg Anyang, built in 2013. Before I got the Beche, the Anyang was the heavy hitter in my shop, and my team and I have used it to make some work that I am very proud of. It's a powerful, reliable, and controllable machine that's never failed us.

This is our 40 kg Anyang C41-15 air hammer. Circa 2013.

This is our 100 lb Little Giant trip hammer. Circa 1953.

THE FORGE

To tell the history of blacksmithing is largely to tell the history of forges. For thousands of years, the fundamental tools of the trade did not change, and indeed, much of the equipment in our shop would be familiar to a medieval village blacksmith. But with every advance in the forge, metal could be produced with greater purity and more consistent material properties while using fewer resources.

The simplest forges appear, on first glance, to be nearly identical to a hearth fire. However, the temperatures needed to heat iron to workable temperatures require the blacksmith to be able to control the flow of air, shape of the fire, and contact with fuel with a greater degree of proficiency than is possible in a hearth. Solving those problems, while also remaining safe, is what has always allowed blacksmiths to succeed.

This shows our four-burner propane forge with a clamshell design. The forge is separate from the firebrick table so it can be lifted to fit larger pieces.

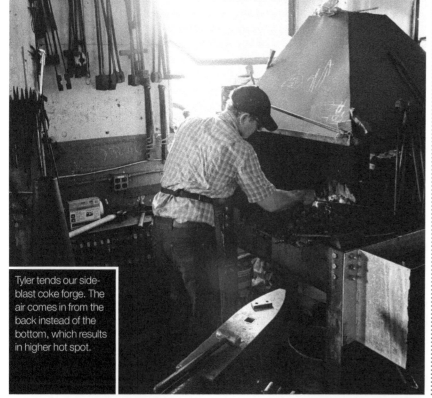

Tyler tends our side-blast coke forge. The air comes in from the back instead of the bottom, which results in higher hot spot.

When I started smithing, I largely used propane, and there are still several propane forges inside my shop for specialized tasks. But I have come to prefer a coke-fired forge for many general forging tasks. Despite coke's dirty reputation, a well-managed coke fire does not smoke or smell. It can be easily managed and shaped with a poker and a rake, allowing me to shape the fire to the metal and use only the fuel I need. And there's nothing like it for fast, intense heating.

Our current forge was designed and built by Matt Garton. It's a side-blast forge, where the air is forced through the fire from the side as opposed to the bottom. Its speed and intensity is partly controlled by the exhaust system. It's an efficient design that concentrates the heat—an important consideration when smithing in the American south.

PRESSES–HYDRAULIC AND FLY

Andrew Chambers uses his custom hydraulic press to hot-punch and drift a hole.

In addition to power hammers, presses can be extremely useful tools in the blacksmith shop. Manual screw-operated fly presses are great general use presses and have some unique advantages over their hydraulic counterparts. Fast-acting hydraulic presses are extremely useful machines for a multitude of heavier forging operations.

The fly press is a manually operated press that predates the hydraulic press. Although they were never popular machines in the States, they were widely used where I was trained in the U.K. They were originally designed for basic stamping and light presswork, but replaced by powered presses in the early 1900s. Since there are very few parts in a fly press that can fail, there are still many useable fly presses floating around the U.K., almost exclusively used by artist blacksmiths.

Beautifully simple in its operation, the fly press uses a large weighted handle to twist a drive screw providing downward force from inertia. Basically, it's a big lever and can depress and return quickly with a push or pull from the operator. Because you have total manual control of the stroke, you can depress the ram gently or forcefully, slowly or quickly. For reliability and ease of use, a fly press can't be

beat. The only downside of the machine is that they usually aren't rated for more than 8 to 10 tons (7,300 to 9,000 kg) of force.

We have three fly presses in our shop: a three ton, a four ton, and six ton deep throat (2,700, 3,600, and 5,400 kg). Our fly presses get used almost every day for both hot and cold work.

If greater force is needed, then a hydraulic press is the answer. Hydraulic forging presses come in all sizes and configurations. Most are either an H frame or a C frame, depending on their intended use and capacity. We have three hydraulic presses in our shop, a 60-ton (54,000 kg) H frame press, a 55-ton (50,000 kg) C frame, and a small horizontal press. The C frame is actually a modified notching machine and is very fast-acting, which makes it great for punching and drifting. The H frame

has a much larger throat but is slightly slower than the C frame and is great for impression work.

The slow action of a press versus a hammer produces a different shaped forging. When a hammer impacts hot steel, it spreads the material from the outside in, spreading the surface first, then the center of the bar. When a press impacts hot steel, the metal moves from the center out like a tube of toothpaste. This difference can create a very different aesthetic when doing operations that only require one deep impression such as a big fuller or ball punch detail.

This is our Sweeney & Blocksidge 8 DB fly press, circa 1910.

HAMMER

Hammers in the form of a stone tied to a stick first appeared in history over 30,000 years ago, and they have advanced very little since then. Even in the world of constant global innovation and technical advancement, it's rare that a structure or machine of any real size or consequence gets produced without the use of some sort of hammer.

In our shop, virtually nothing is made without the use of a hammer. We treat the hammer with reverence: the sort of reverence earned from contributing to 30,000 years of human achievement. We have hundreds of hammers—most are made, some are bought. Most of them have a story. Some of them were made on the other side of the globe by friends of ours and embody their personal style and attitude toward forging. Many of them were forged by Matt on a Saturday afternoon or during a hammer-making workshop. They are all different in their own way, but also all very effective in the right hands.

In England, parts of Europe, and North America, many smiths opt for a lighter hammer on a long, thin handle. Their theory is that velocity is most important and high velocity can be best achieved using a longer handle and creating a larger arc in your swing. In Eastern Europe and the Middle East, they believe the opposite—that mass is most important—thus they use heavier hammers on shorter handles. This school of thought hinges on the idea that more mass hits with more energy and leads to getting the job done in fewer blows.

There seems to be a lot of debate about what sort of hammer works best, but I think that is an impossible question to answer.

There are hundreds, maybe thousands, of different shapes and sizes of hammers used regularly and successfully by blacksmiths around the world. Some are heavy, some are light, some have long handles, and some are short.

In some workshops that do very specific and repetitive hand forging, specific hammer shape and weight can be very important. As a shop that does a variety of complex work, we have hammers of all shapes and sizes and we use them all. We use short-handled, 4 pound (1.8 kg) Czech-style hammers and long-handled 2 pound (0.9 kg) ball peens, often on the same project. I usually work with whatever hammer I'm feeling most comfortable with and that changes frequently.

TONGS

Pete Smith, one of my forging instructors in Hereford, always said, "If you can't hold it, you can't forge it." He always preached the importance of having the right size tongs for every shape and size of material so you could concentrate on forging rather than stabilizing material. He was absolutely right. We keep about 200 sets of tongs on various racks throughout the shop to make sure we can always grip the material we are trying to forge. For many jobs, the first step is forging a specific set of tongs to hold the material.

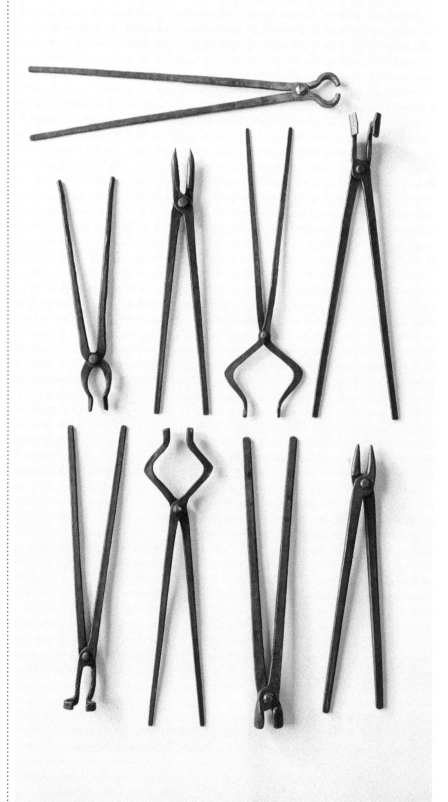

PUNCH

There are many different ways to punch a hole through a bar of hot steel. We keep a large assortment of round, square, slitting, and slot punches in our shop. Since different styles of punches produce different results, there is no one type of punch that is superior, just different.

A round punch is usually used in lieu of drilling to produce a similar result: maximum stock removal and minimal deformation around the hole. A square punch is usually used to produce a square hole with minimum outside deformation. When a hole or joint is not meant to be highlighted, the round and square punches are a good choice.

When a hole *is* intended to be highlighted, a punch can be useful to deform the outside material as much as possible. Making a hole that is a long oval or slit and then drifting it open to either a round or square hole causes the outside material to swell out around the hole and create a point of design interest. This type of hole also makes for a stronger connection since more material is left on the sides of the hole. The most dramatic swelled holes are created with slitting punches since little or no material is removed and everything is displaced to the sides of the hole. Drifting a slit hole requires a great deal of force because the hole actually needs to be stretched open.

The next most dramatic swells are created using a slot punch. The slot punch creates an oval or rectangular hole that usually has the same circumference as the intended finished hole. The hole is reshaped by the drift rather than stretched as with the slitting punch. The resulting shape is a significant swell of material around the hole; it's nearly as significant as the slitting punch in most cases. The combination of aesthetics and ease of drifting makes the slot punch our most often used style of punch by far. We have hundreds of different slot punches in different sizes and shapes. Some have wood handles, some are handheld, and some are held with dedicated tongs.

DRIFT

Once most holes are punched, the next step is to open them up to a specific size or shape. For that, a drift is used. In some cases, as with the cheeks of a hammer for instance, a drift can also be used to bolster material being forged. This is done by forging the sides of a hole with the drift left inside to maintain the shape of the hole. We custom make our drifts for specific hole sizes and projects. Some drifts that are only needed for a few holes may be made of mild steel and case-hardened. For drifts that will be used regularly, we use high carbon or alloy steel with a high hardness rating.

CHISEL

In the days before band saws or even hacksaws, a chisel was the only option for cutting metal. Nowadays, we have many cutting options at our disposal, but we still often use the chisel, especially for cutting bars hot. Simply cutting off a hot bar at the anvil or under the power hammer is much faster than waiting for it to cool, cutting it on the saw, and heating it back up to forging temperature. The downside of cutting with a hot chisel is a loss in cut accuracy.

We also make use of many different chisels for chasing and decorative operations. We use handheld and wood-handled chisels in many different shapes and sizes for different effects.

SET HAMMER

The set hammer is an extremely useful tool, especially when doing work with abrupt sectional changes and redirections. The set hammer is a top tool that has a flat, square face with slightly radiused edged to get into sharp corners. We use set hammers all the time in conjunction with flatters.

FLATTER

The flatter is a traditional blacksmithing top tool (see page 56) likely found in some form in most shops in the world. We use wood-handled flatters at the anvil and low-profile, round-backed flatters under the power hammer. Both are extremely useful, especially when tapering material using flat dies as they easily remove any unwanted hammer marks.

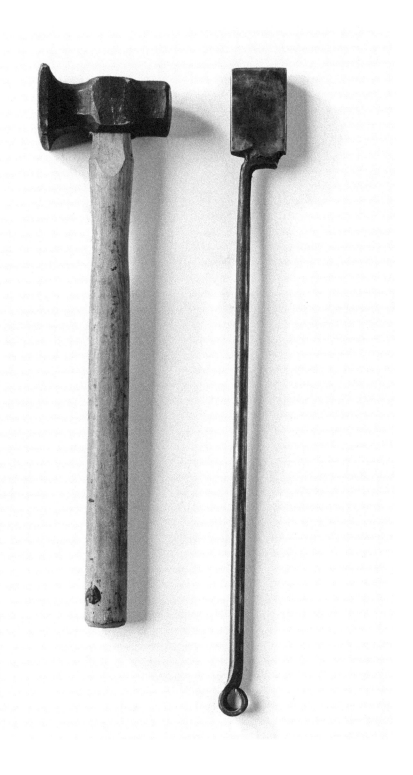

TOP AND BOTTOM FULLER

A top and bottom refers to paired set of tools with the top tool being a handled tool and the bottom tool being a hardy tool with a matching profile. A set of matching top and bottom fullers can be extremely useful in many different operations such as hammer-making, tong-making, and really any type of material isolation. We make these matching sets often as we need a slightly different radius for different projects.

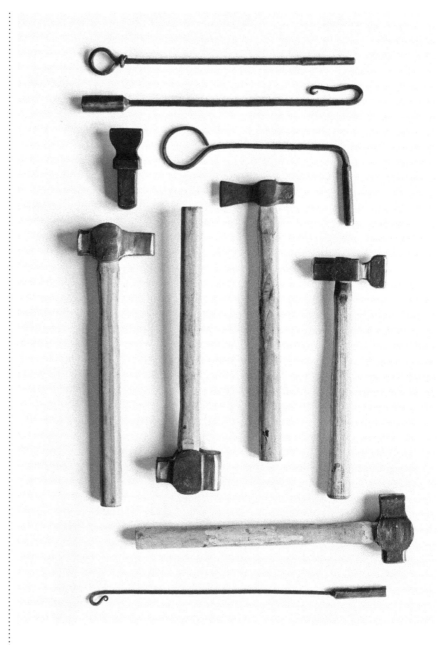

OTHER MACHINERY AND EQUIPMENT

LAYOUT TABLES

The importance of having a sturdy, flat work surface in the shop cannot be overstated. When assembling a project, reference points are needed to line things up and make sure they're level (if they need to be). We find that the ideal reference plane for most project assembly procedures is the surface of the table on which we're building. We use three main types of layout tables in the shop: steel, platen, and trellis (not exactly a table, but sort of).

We have several steel tables in various shapes and sizes, with varying plate thicknesses for the table tops. One of the advantages of working on a steel table is the ability to draw a design directly on the surface of the table. This can be a real time saver when working on short projects that won't monopolize the table surface for too long. If the table gets used for too many other projects, the drawing tends to disappear. We use a cheap clear coat to cover important drawings we want to keep.

Another great aspect of building on steel tables is having the ability to weld fixtures directly to the table's surface. We try to avoid welding to the table whenever possible, but it can be very handy in some situations. A distinct disadvantage of the steel table is that very hot work pieces can warp the steel unless it's incredibly thick. Cost is also an important consideration with layout tables. Any good table will be expensive, but fabricating your own steel table with a heavy tube or angle frame is the most cost-effective option.

A platen table is table that consists of a cast iron platen on a table-height stand. Originally developed for the fabrication and manufacturing industries, a platen is a thick, cast iron work surface with square holes at regular intervals throughout. They are machined totally flat from the factory and cast 3 to 5 inches (76 to 127 mm) thick to ensure that they won't bend or warp even under great heat and stress. Because of their stout design and heat resistance, platens lend themselves to blacksmith work extremely well.

We have a 5 by 7 foot (1.5 × 2 m) cast iron platen table, and it's one of the most important tools in the shop. We use ours for bending, straightening, restraining, layout, and setup. We also have many custom fixtures and tooling setups that attach to the platen. Simply clamping a piece to the work surface is fast and secure using basic hold-downs we make ourselves out of 1½" (38 mm) round bar. These tension-fit clamps generate an enormous amount of clamping pressure and can be put in and removed with a few blows of the sledge hammer—simple engineering at its finest. We also have vertical twist clamps for more precise work holding.

Some disadvantages of the platen table are price and layout versatility. We got ours from our local scrap yard for scrap price, but at about 4,000 pounds (1,800 kg), that still wasn't cheap! The good news is, being that they are chunks of cast iron weighing multiple tons, these things tend to last quite a while. The other main disadvantage of using a platen table as your main working surface

Here's our 5 by 7 foot (1.5 × 2 m) platen table with clamps and hold-downs with a 3 by 9 foot (1 × 3 m) steel table on large wheels in the background.

is the inability to draw a design directly on the table. We will often do our drawings on thinner steel plates that sit on the platen table. This works okay, but they inevitably end up warping due to the heat and then the dimensions can no longer be trusted.

For larger projects, we often use heavy steel trellises either on their own or in conjunction with our other tables. All tables and trellises are built to the same height so we can stretch projects across multiple work surfaces if necessary. Our trellises are built extremely stout, with wide steel plates welded to heavy I-beams forming the work surface. For small projects, they can be used on their own as little layout tables.

The style of a shop's layout tables is a function of project size and available space. In my travels, I have seen tables of all shapes and sizes. When it comes to layout tables, there is no one style of table that works for every project. We find it very useful to have several different table options since every project is different.

SLACK TUB

Derived from the word slake—*to quench*, the slack tub is a tub of water used to quench hot material. The slack tub is a simple but essential element of any working forge. Even the most modest forges have a pail of water not far from the fire. Because complex and large forgings often require localized quenching in awkward places, we have several different slack tubs of varying size and shape, from a 48 by 10 by 20 inch (1219 × 254 × 508 mm) galvanized steel tub on down to the trusty five-gallon (19 L) pail.

POST VISE

Often called a leg vise or blacksmith's vise, the post vise is an indispensable tool for the blacksmith shop. We use ours to hold material tightly while we twist, upset, chisel, bend, straighten, grind, and file it. The post vise is designed to be extremely stout and stand up to daily abuse from all those operations and more. Post vises have a distinctive post or leg that extends all the way down to the ground when the vise is mounted at working height. The post absorbs the impact of hammering and directs the energy into the ground rather than stressing the stand or table to which the vise is attached. They also have a very

heavy but loosely fitted screw to provide the clamping pressure. Having the screw loosely fitted allows the jaws to have some play and be able to twist slightly to grab pieces without completely parallel sides. Once the screw is tightened, the pressure holds the jaws in line.

The best post vises are forged, not cast. Their forged construction makes them much more durable and impact resistant. Forging a post vise is an extremely difficult task and great exercise in mass isolation. The post vise is such an advanced forging project that it was often the final project an apprentice

would complete before they were given the title of journeyman in the craft guild hierarchies of old.

We have several post vises of varying shapes and sizes set up in our shop. Since there always seems to be a need to hold something securely, we have them scattered throughout the shop with the largest ones near the forging areas.

SWAGE BLOCK

A swage block is a classic piece of traditional blacksmith tooling. It's an extremely versatile piece of tooling and something we use very often. The holes work great as bolsters and as areas to dish or form material. The V grooves on the side work well to create sharp angles and bend things like tong jaws.

WELDING/GRINDING EQUIPMENT

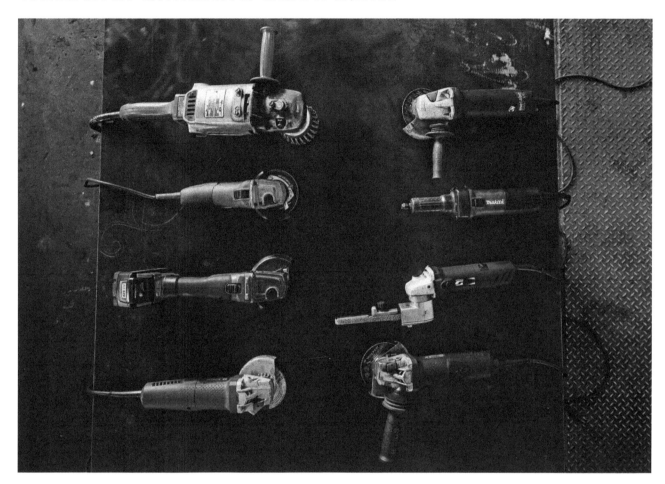

Welding and grinding are far from the most enjoyable tasks in the shop, but they are a necessary step for many projects. In tool and fixture making, modern fabrication is often the best way to get the job done. It's always rewarding to forge something, but if an identical form can be created quicker through fabrication, I will usually opt to fabricate it. This is especially true for commissioned work. The way we can offer our customers value is to offer them something they cannot get anywhere else—offer them something very obviously forged. If a certain element is not meant to look forged, then perhaps it shouldn't be. Adding forge time for parts that won't be visible steals from time that could be spent highlighting the forging process where

it is meant to be seen. We fabricate that which won't be noticed so we can spend time forging that which will.

In order to carry out this fabrication, we have several welding machines in the shop and a few portable machines for installation work. Our main production welder is a big, old 350A MIG (metal inert gas) machine with a separate power supply and jib-mounted wire feeder. We also have some smaller MIG machines throughout the shop to be used in the areas where the jib won't reach. We have TIG (tungsten inert gas) and arc welders as well, although we rarely use them. The TIG gets used often when we work with nonferrous metals like silicon bronze. We use the arc welder when working with antique wrought and cast iron on

restoration projects. For installation work, we usually use portable MIG welders with flux-core wire.

For grinding and finishing, we use variable speed angle grinders, die grinders, belt sanders, and hand files.

DRILL PRESS

Our drill press gets quite a bit of use because we often try to incorporate riveted joinery even if a project's budget and time constraints don't allow for hot-punched holes. In these cases, drilled holes with rivet connections are a nice compromise because they still make the design statement of a mechanical connection without being very time-consuming. In many cases, drilling and riveting can be just as fast as a welding and cleaning the same joint.

Our drill press is a Portuguese machine produced some time in the mid 1980s. It's a great machine with lots of adjustability and variable speeds. The big advantage of this drill press is that it is gear driven, rather than belt driven. After having a few, we prefer the gear drive because it doesn't slip under heavy torque.

BAND SAWS

Since every bar we forge must be cut, the most popular machine in the shop is probably the horizontal band saw. It's a wet-cut saw that has single mitering capability and hydraulic auto-drop. It's not the prettiest machine in the shop, but I don't know what we'd do without it. A well calibrated saw to make consistent cuts is essential in production work.

The vertical band saw is also a very useful tool although not as essential as the horizontal. We use ours for cutting small or oddly shaped parts all the time. It's also handy for making curved and deep cuts.

For versatility, the portable band saw or port-a-band is awesome. We have corded and cordless port-a-bands that get used every day. They are super useful and versatile tools to have on an installation site as well.

OTHER FABRICATION MACHINES

Over the years of equipment auctions and scrap yard finds, we have accumulated a nice collection of other general fabrication machinery. We've even had to break down and buy some of it new. Some of these machines are modified in some way to work better for blacksmith work, but most are left stock.

One such machine is a 40-ton (36,000 kg) rated hydraulic angle rolling machine. This machine creates constant-radius arcs in standard, cold, steel bars. Creating the shapes in this way rather than hot forming is another example of an opportunity to add value to a project without compromising quality. As long as the intended results are the same, curving a bar with the rolling machine may afford us the opportunity to add more interesting forging to another part of a project using the time saved.

We also have a 55-ton (50,000 kg) ironworker that came to us missing the notcher assembly. Rather than replacing the notching setup, we built a fixture that allows us to hot punch holes in material up to 3 inch (76 mm) square with ease. Hot-punched holes are an important part of our in-house design style, but they can also be very time-consuming and labor-intensive to create by hand. Having a dedicated hydraulic punching station allows us to streamline the process and incorporate more punched holes in our work.

We have various bench grinders, belt sanders, and other small metalworking machines as well, all of which we are constantly finding new, creative uses for.

JP smooths out a forging in front of our angle roller that's in the background.

TOOL RACKS

Proper racking is an essential part of any shop. With multiple people working at the same time, it's important to know where you can find something. A good blacksmith is constantly improving not only their skill set, but also their tooling and work environment. All those tools need somewhere to go. Good racking can be the difference between a shop that feels small and cluttered and a shop that feels like a place where creativity can flourish.

We try to have racking for tools as close to the place of their intended use as possible. Making it easy to put tools away means they will more often find their way to their rightful home. For instance, there is a power hammer tool rack hanging on the front of the power hammer so it's always in arm's reach of the operator.

TECHNIQUES

HE IS A POOR CRAFTSMAN WHO BRINGS
HIS HEATED IRON BELOW THE HAMMER
WITH NO CLEAR IDEA IN HIS HEAD AS TO
WHAT HE INTENDS TO DO FIRST.

J.W. Lillico, *Blacksmith's Manual Illustrated*

LAYOUT

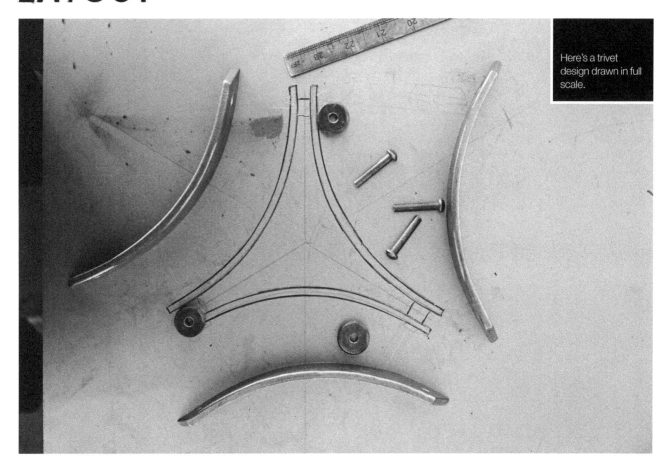

Here's a trivet design drawn in full scale.

The first step in any project of reasonable complexity is to create a full-sized layout drawing to use for reference. Unlike carpentry work, which generally deals with straight lines, square corners, and parts spaced at regular intervals, decorative ironwork has unique design concerns that must be drawn in full scale to be defined. To stay on the carpentry analogy: Where a carpenter cuts boards and joins them together, a great deal of the work of a blacksmith lies in actually making the boards, or in our case, bars. Most architectural projects like gates and railings break down to about a fifty/fifty division of time spent forging parts versus assembling them. Having an accurate full-scale drawing enables you to have a reference point from which to match parts and assemble them.

A square, flat, steel layout table is my preferred surface. Designs can be drawn directly onto a steel layout table, a loose steel plate, or even a concrete floor. Non-flammable surfaces work best; you can lay the hot bars directly onto the drawing without lighting the drawing on fire. A good trick to keep a new drawing from getting wiped away in a busy workshop is to spray the lines with a clear-coat after drawing them.

Many people also use wood or MDF sheets painted white because you can easily move these around and paint over them when it's time for the next project. With layout methods like these, you must be careful not to touch the hot parts of the metal to the drawing surface. The metal will burn the drawing.

When moving from a paper drawing to full-scale project layout, there is ample opportunity for mistakes to happen. This is the part of the project where you need to be exact and positive that the measurements are correct. A mistake made here will always result in rework. It is for this reason that many commercial architectural blacksmiths and fabricators are moving toward using large format plotters to print out railing drawings in full scale. It is much harder to make an error this way, and if you burn up the drawing, you can always print out another.

HAND FORGING

Hand forging refers to any forging process done at the anvil with a hand hammer and/or a striker. Proficiency at hand forging is an absolute necessity to any forging practice. Eventually, you'll find that you can use many different tools and machines such as power hammers and presses to achieve the same forged form. By jumping to the use of these machines before fully grasping the hand forged process, you compromise your understanding of the process.

A strong understanding of handwork at the anvil will be the core of your practice and something you'll always be able to come back to no matter what direction your work goes in. In my shop, we do much of our rough forging on the power hammer and refine the shapes at the anvil. Working back and forth in harmony with the machines, we can get a lot of work done, but keep the forms fun and interesting.

HAND FORMING

The evolution of a finished piece of forge work usually goes as follows: forging, then forming, and then assembly (if multiple pieces) and finish. The forging process molds the material into a different cross-sectional dimension than it started. After a piece is forged to a particular dimension, it will often need to be formed into a different shape by bending or twisting in two- and three-dimensional space. Forging and forming often happen simultaneously, but they are two different processes. Forming can be done either free form without any guides or jigs or around a jig or former. Forming also often means simply straightening or correcting a piece that has been bent during the forging process.

Two-dimensional forming can be done to match a full-scale layout drawing. Three-dimensional (3-D) forming is more complicated and involves a degree of finesse and artistic eye to execute successfully. There are often very few reference points to use when matching a 3-D form. The smith has to rely on their own understanding of scale, dimension, proportion, and other abstract design properties. For this reason, many smiths find 3-D forming to be one of the more difficult aspects of their practice.

There are a number of different tools that can be used for forming metal in three dimensions, but most smiths have their preferences. I find myself using anvil forks often for all sorts of 3-D forming operations. They are versatile and can be used with handheld bending forks or with the hammer to achieve various bends. By holding the workpiece at different angles through the fork, you can add a twist to your bends or quickly change the plane in which you are bending. I also often use the fly press with a three point bending setup and a cone mandrel.

John Winer uses the cone mandrel to refine a long curve. The cone mandrel is an excellent tool for three-dimensional forming.

The thing about 3-D forming is that it's hard to get right and very easy to get wrong. There's no special tool or jig that will take judgment and experience out of the equation. Many blacksmiths only design projects free of 3-D forms to avoid this type of work. Other smiths, like Albert Paley, John Medwedeff, or Michael Dillon, often work in 3-D and do it well. It's one of those things that will take a whole lot of practice, but in that practice, you'll gain a much deeper understanding of the limitations of metal.

POWER HAMMER WORK

The world in which the great blacksmiths of the past like Samuel Yellin or Alessandro Mazzucotelli made their masterpieces was a very different place. Their great works were created in a time when skilled labor was cheap and plentiful. Nowadays, it's not economically feasible or ethically responsible to exploit cheap labor the way it was done 100 years ago. So, the modern smith must exploit the use of technology to get the job done.

Of course, we still try to hire and train as many enthusiastic blacksmiths as possible. The American College of Building Arts (ACBA) is a college here in Charleston that offers a four-year degree program in architectural ironwork. The ACBA program develops a solid foundation in forgework, design drafting, and even preservation. We work closely with the college to hire and train interns every summer and in some cases, hire them full time when they graduate. There are very few programs in the country like this, so we are fortunate to be located right in the same town.

In addition to the multitude of skilled labor, the old masters also had the advantage of using wrought iron as their primary material. Compared to the steel we use today, wrought iron is a much more malleable metal and thus requires less energy to forge. In order to leave their own indelible mark on the world, the modern smith uses a machine to move as much metal as possible. More often than not, that machine is a power hammer.

The importance of the power hammer to modern blacksmith work cannot be understated. Without one, it's very difficult to produce large work on your own. The power hammer is one of the greatest engineering triumphs of the modern world, and most blacksmiths treat theirs with reverence and respect: meticulously maintaining them, naming them, and even giving them custom paint jobs. Power hammers are designed to forge large sections of bar quickly and can be unforgiving if not controlled properly. They should be used with concentration and care to ensure the safety of the operator and the quality of the work.

There are two main types of power hammer work: open die forging and closed die forging. Open die forging refers to hot forging between dies that are not completely closed, usually flat dies. Closed die forging involves hot forging between two dies that are completely closed and thus results in a specific shape produced every time. The modern blacksmith mostly uses open die forging techniques but sometimes employs closed die forging in the form of swages or custom power hammer dies.

It's important to remember that any form created at the anvil with a hand hammer can also be created using a power hammer. The top die is often referred to as the hammerhead and the bottom die as the anvil because that's what they are. Different shaped dies such as fullering, drawing, and crowning are often used to produce different shapes, although many smiths achieve the same shapes using tooling and swages between flat dies. In my opinion, large, flat dies with radiused corners are the most versatile. Well-appointed forges often have multiple power hammers with different dies for different jobs, so you can move between operations without stopping to change dies.

It's not uncommon for a blacksmith to have hundreds or even thousands of power hammer tools and swages. The multitude of power hammer tools you'll find when searching for tooling ideas can seem overwhelming. You can achieve many different complex forgings using a few basic pieces of tooling that can be made in an afternoon.

Quite possibly, my most often used power hammer tool is the round back flatter. This is a low profile flatter that has a radiused back to it that can be used for fullering and spreading material. By flipping this tool, you can quickly spread material and then smooth it out. Because the tool is much smaller than the face of the upper die, it concentrates the energy of the blow so that a great deal of material can be moved quickly. One of the main drawbacks of using flat dies is that you end up with an uneven, stepped surface when forging anything that doesn't have parallel sides, such as a tapered bar. The roundback flatter can be used to smooth out the surface of an uneven forging. Because of the rounded back of the tool, it can be held flat to a sloped surface.

Another very important tool is the side set tool. The side set has a triangular profile and is used to precisely isolate mass and create extreme changes in sectional dimension.

The third tool is a cutter or sometimes called a hack tool. This is a sharper version of the side set that is designed specifically to cut off material. Using the cutter, you can cut off a forging and keep working without waiting for the bar to cool down so you can use the saw. All three of these tools should be made with very thin handles (no more than ⅓ inch [9 mm] round). Using the thin bar stock as handle material will save your hand

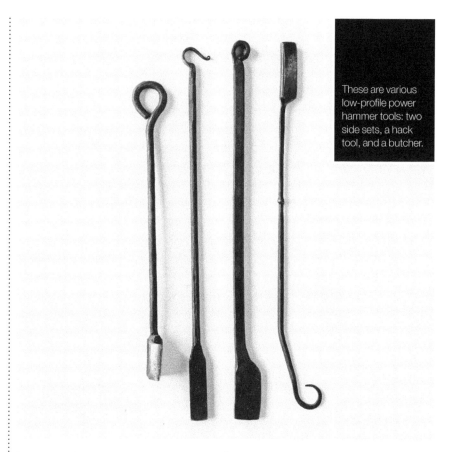

These are various low-profile power hammer tools: two side sets, a hack tool, and a butcher.

from a lot of pain if the tool is not aligned properly because the handle will bend rather than your arm.

One of the main advantages of using a power hammer is that you're able to create a form using less heats than doing it by hand or even with a striker. Finishing your work in less heats not only has the advantage of time and cost savings, but the work will look better. Many of the forms created by the modern smith highlight sections of the material that have not been directly impacted with tooling, such as the swell bulged out around a drifted hole. Since these surfaces cannot be reforged or planished, they must be protected from surface deterioration caused by overheating. The best way to keep these surfaces protected is to get the job

done in the minimum amount of heats. Clear thinking ahead of time and proper tooling will result in the creation of a form in fewer heats.

After the initial principles of safe power hammer use are grasped, the possibilities are nearly endless. Since tooling can be made in-house and be simple or complicated, it's no surprise that smiths seem to be coming up with new ways to create forms all the time. Die saddles with tooling holders are extremely useful and make it quick and easy to make tooling that can be held securely in place. Tooling innovation allows for forms previously thought to be too time-consuming for a particular project to be made quicker, which drives the craft forward.

HOLE PUNCHING

Before the drill bit was invented, there was only one way to get a hole in piece of iron: by punching. Hot punching involves driving a tool called a punch through a hot bar to create a hole. The hole is then usually opened to a specific size with a drift. Now, there are many different ways to make a hole through a bar of steel—cold punching, drilling, laser cutting, and plasma cutting—all of which are less physical work and more precise. There are two main advantages to hot punching your holes: aesthetics and strength. Most hot-punched holes have a swell around the hole after it's sized that makes for beautiful joinery detail. The swell is caused by material being spread out of the way of a hole rather than removed as it is in the aforementioned modern hole making methods. Since more material is left around the hole, the bar is left stronger. Another advantage is speed; just as with hot cutting, time is saved by not waiting for the steel to cool.

Holes can be punched using different shaped punches to achieve various finished hole shapes and sizes. Punch geometry for different applications is an often-debated subject, but ultimately comes down to personal preference since there are distinct advantages and disadvantages of every type of punch. Being trained in England, I most often use a slot punch since the English traditionally use this type of punch almost exclusively. In Israel and in many American forges, smiths seem to favor slitting punches for many applications. There is no one type of punch that is best for everything, so it's a good idea to have a variety of punches in your toolbox.

In addition to tip geometry, there are also many different options when it comes to holding and driving a punch.

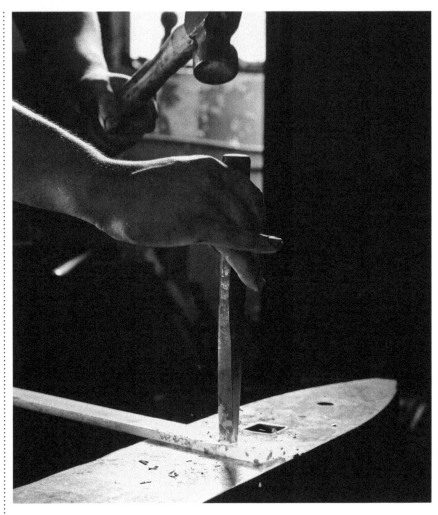

The simplest way to punch a hole is by holding a handheld punch in one hand and striking it with a hand hammer in the other. For larger pieces especially, some smiths prefer using handled punches that either have a wooden handle or are held in special tongs. Handled punches are the type used under power hammers. Many smiths also use hydraulic and fly presses to punch holes.

DRIFTING

Drifting is a the process of opening a hole to a specific size by driving a tool called a drift through the hole. A drift is a tapered tool that gradually opens a hole as it passes through. Drifts can be round, square, oval, oblong, or any other of a number of various shapes used for unique applications. Drifting is usually done at the anvil either by hand or with the assistance of a striker, although it can be done with a power hammer or press using special tooling. It's important to make sure that the material is supported around the area of the hole with a suitable bolster to prevent the drift from dragging, unless that's your goal. Drifts don't need to be extremely hard, and mild steel will often work just fine as drift material. It is important that the drift is as smooth as possible because the drifting process involves so much friction. The punch and drift can be combined into a single tool.

This is an examle of drifting a slot-punched hole into a rectangle using a rectangular drift.

FULLERING, SPREADING, AND ISOLATION

This shows spreading material at the anvil using a handled fuller with a striker.

Here, a spring fuller is used under the power hammer to isolate material.

The fuller dies can create dramatic shapes when used for spreading operations.

This is a close-up view of a sculptural piece by John Winer. It's a great example of spreading with a fuller.

When the surface hitting the hot metal is flat, such as in the case of the flat side of the hammer or the flat die on a power hammer, the material moves equally in all directions. When the metal is contacted by a curved surface, or fuller, such as a fullering die, cross peen of a hammer, or a fuller top tool, the metal can be directed out in one direction: in this case, perpendicular to the fuller or peen direction.

Fullering is a technique often used to make artistic or sculptural forms. Because of the sharpness of a fuller when it impacts the material, it can create a dramatic change in section and direct material drastically away from its original configuration. The violent impact of the fuller leaves a deep texture, and this can either be smoothed out with a flatter or left as a design feature. Drastically fullered textures and forms are a design feature found in the work of many contemporary smiths but rarely found in the work of traditional smiths. Although traditional smiths use fullers all the time, the work is usually smoothed out after the fullering process.

While fullers attached to the top die of the power hammer or on the peen of the hammer are useful for spreading or fanning out material, a handheld fuller is great to leave a single, deep impression to separate or isolate mass. The stylistic possibilities of isolating sections with deep fullers are nearly endless, and that's why fullering in all its forms is such an intriguing technique for the modern smith.

TAPERING OR DRAWING DOWN

Tapering is the most basic forging process but also possibly the most often employed, depending on your style. Tapering refers to the process of stretching, or drawing out, a bar while shrinking the cross-sectional dimension of the bar. A tapered point makes for a visually appealing termination to a bar, although it's not the only way to make an aesthetically pleasing termination. Tapering is achieved by forging a bar in two different directions and can be done either with the flat or fullering dies.

This shows drawing out a long taper on the power hammer.

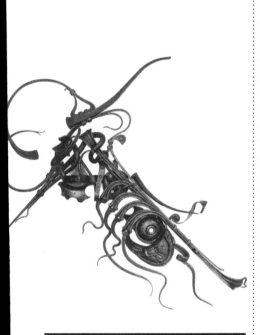

Conception through Assention by John Winer. This is a wall sculpture that incorporates many tapered bars with multiple other forms to create a very unique aesthetic, and a beautiful piece. Fine tapers like these require very controlled forging and forming.

UPSETTING

Upsetting is essentially the opposite of tapering a bar. The material is driven back into itself, effectively shortening the bar. The material needs somewhere to go when it's driven back into itself, and it ends up flaring out and widening the end of the bar. Although there are many structural reasons to upset, many times a bar is upset for aesthetics. Like a tapered end, an upset end makes a very appealing termination for a bar. Upsetting can also be a controlled process used to create mass in the center of bar by quenching the end of the bar before upsetting, thus expanding the material in the hottest point, which may not be the end of the bar.

Here a ground anvil is used to upset a bar. The mass of the bar acts as the hammer.

Here's a very unique lamp base by James Price. The circular ring was created by drastically upsetting a round bar and letting the material bulge out.

TENON MAKING

An important design feature for many contemporary projects including those in this book is the mortise-and-tenon joint. The hole punching and drifting techniques described earlier are used to create the mortise. Alternatively, the hole could be drilled, but this is less desirable aesthetically. A tenon is essentially a rivet attached to the end of a bar that's used to connect to another bar.

Making a tenon is a multi-step process that takes some practice to gain proficiency. The first step to create a tenon is to establish a shoulder and section off material for the tenon. The shoulder acts as the backing for the connection and should be established precisely and squarely. The shoulder should be cut in on all sides using a butchering tool, which is a sharp, offset fuller used to section off material. Butchering tools can be used at the anvil by hand, under a power hammer, or even with a press.

After the section of bar that is to be the tenon is isolated on the end of a bar, it needs to be forged into the desired shape to correspond with the mortise. This can be done by hand or on the power hammer, and the shape is often finished using a swage of the proper size.

The last step of the tenon making process is refining the shoulder using a monkey tool to drive material back into the bar and create a square shoulder. The shape can be further refined with file work if necessary.

Once complete, the tenon is mated to a mortise and hammered over just like a rivet head, creating a strong and beautiful connection.

This shows using a butchering swage under the power hammer. The swage has two guide pins to keep the butchers directly in line.

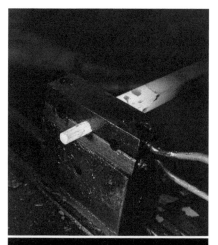

This shows using a tenon swage to forge tenons down to a desired size. It is a simple swage with guides.

This is the last step of tenon forging. A monkey tool is used to square the shoulders of the bar.

CHASING

Chasing is the process of creating decorative lines and impressions into the surface of the material using chisels and fullers. Chisels and fullers of all shapes and sizes can be used by hand, with the power hammer, or press. Often associated with repoussé, chasing is a widely used technique in traditional and historical blacksmithing, but it also has its place in contemporary work.

REPOUSSÉ

Repoussé is a form of metalworking that involves forming a design by alternating between hitting from the front and reverse side of a workpiece. It's a technique usually associated with classical and traditional metalwork, but there are many creative applications for the contemporary blacksmith. Repoussé can be performed cold or hot depending on the material and whether or not it has been annealed. Incorporating repoussé into a project offers great opportunity to introduce another metal like copper or bronze into a design.

Matt works on a copper goblin face using classic repoussé techniques.

RIVETING

These are large custom-made rivets forged by Steve Howell.

Smaller rivets can be hammered cold, especially if they're annealed beforehand.

Adrian Legge, the head forging professor at the National School of Blacksmithing in Hereford, England, has a dog named Rivet. Adrian is always happy to explain that he chose the name Rivet because the rivet is the most useful thing in the blacksmith shop.

A rivet is one of the oldest and strongest fasteners. A rivet creates a permanent attachment between two surfaces that can hold a great load in both shear and tension applications. There are many different types of rivets, but the type most often used in the work of the modern blacksmith is a solid rivet. Solid rivets have been around for millennia, dating back to at least the Bronze Age and possibly even longer. A solid rivet is still one of the most secure ways of mechanically fastening things together.

Solid rivets became widely used during the industrial revolution when mass production allowed for structural steel projects to get much larger than they had previously been. The solid rivet is traditionally made up of a domed head on top of a cylindrical shaft. During the riveting process, the shaft of the rivet is heated to a malleable state and upset to compress two substrates together. The bond between the two pieces gets tighter as the rivet cools and contracts.

From an aesthetic standpoint, the rivet is still an almost universally understood symbol of industrial strength and durability. Many iconic examples of exceptional design and engineering are defined by their heavily riveted components. From the Golden Gate Bridge to the Eiffel Tower, our world is full of riveted structures defined by beauty and permanence.

Today, there are many ways to join two bars of metal together. A craftsperson chooses to use a rivet for reasons of pride or beauty. The rivet tells a story of strength and precision. For the modern smith, the rivet is pure and basic; it's a design statement that screams timeless craftsmanship while giving a subtle nod to the masters of the past.

A steel truss is being riveted together using a large hydraulic riveting press at Ballard Forge, Steve Howell's workshop in Seattle, Washington.

FORGE WELDING

Until the invention of the electric welding machine in the late nineteenth century, the only way to weld two pieces of metal together was using fire. Since the dawn of the Iron Age, there have been smiths using this technique to join bars together. Forge welding is simple in practice but often difficult to achieve because of a very specific set of parameters.

The pieces that are to be welded are heated to a bright, yellow-white heat at which point the surface becomes molten. The molten pieces are lightly hammered together until they stick and are fused into one piece. Because some material is burned away during the forge welding process, it's easy to forge your weld too thin after the fusion has taken place. To counteract this, it's important to upset both welded surfaces prior to welding to allow for some shrinkage.

Forge welding can be a useful skill and with some practice, it can become a faster alternative to electric welding in some situations. Time is saved by forge welding parts at the anvil rather than waiting for them to cool and then prepping, electric welding, and grinding the same joint.

FINISHING

The finishing process takes a good piece and makes it great. There are a seemingly infinite number of finishes that can be applied to forged steel. Different projects call for different finishes, so it's very helpful to keep an open mind and never get too set on using any one finish for everything.

There are many more options for interior work than for exterior work because the risk of corrosion is far less with interior work. The reality is that in most climates, rust is inevitable if steel is left unfinished, even if the piece is indoors. The primary objective of finishing is protection, and many beautiful finishes have been born out of necessity.

Because there are far more finishing options than can be described here, I'll focus on a few that have given me great results.

The first step of most finishing processes is surface preparation. Forging creates a layer of scale on the surface of the metal that must be removed before most finishes applied. The degree to which you must clean the surface depends on the finish you want to create. If you're going for a dark, natural looking finish on interior ironwork, you may opt to only remove the loose fire scale. If you're applying a patina or painting the surface, you may want to clean the entire surface to a white steel. There are quite a few different methods of surface cleaning. Cleaning can be done by wire wheel, sanding, sandblasting, tumbling, or by etching the surface with acid.

Interior ironwork can be colored with patina or with the use of heat before being coated. If there are ground welds or other areas of discolor, we use darkening solution to blend the colors.

Most of our interior work is then coated with either wax or lacquer. Many people also use linseed oil, shellac, and paint finishes.

Because of the harsh coastal climate here in Charleston, South Carolina, almost all of our exterior ironwork is galvanized. Galvanizing is a process of adhering a layer of molten zinc to the surface of the ironwork by dipping it into a zinc bath.

HEAT TREATMENT

Heat treatment refers to the heating and cooling of steel to alter the physical characteristics of the material. For the practical purposes of blacksmithing and toolmaking, this usually means hardening or softening, simultaneously affecting the strength and toughness. This treatment is performed through controlled cooling and heating of the material.

One of the greatest and most fulfilling aspects of a blacksmith practice is the ability and often necessity to make your own tools. In our shop, we create many of our own tools and often end up having to heat-treat steels and alloys. The development of many modern alloys and tool steels in the twentieth century has given a great advantage to the modern smith when it comes to tool effectiveness and durability.

At a molecular level, many changes occur to the grain structure of the material during the heat treatment process, resulting in harder or softer tool surfaces. Explaining the science behind these changes could be a book on its own, so we won't get into the details here. There are usually three important steps to heat-treating a tool: annealing, hardening, and tempering.

Annealing is a process by which metal is heated to a determined temperature and then cooled slowly to refine and relax the grain structure. This results in a part that is soft and ductile. Annealed parts are easier to cold-bend and machine. The forging process itself is a form of heat treatment that changes properties of the material, whether or not it's intended. After a part is forged, it must be annealed prior to hardening to allow for an even and consistent hardening process.

Hardening involves rapidly cooling the metal to hold the grain structure at a specific size and configuration, resulting in a harder but often more

brittle part. The rapid cooling is done by quenching the material. It is either dipped in water or oil or left to air cool, depending on the type of steel or alloy. This is a very specific process for each different material. Hardening can also be achieved through a process called case-hardening where a carburizing compound is spread on the surface of the metal and allowed to diffuse into the surface at high temperature. This results in a thin layer of hardened material on the case-hardened surface.

When a piece of steel is hardened, its initial state is usually very hard but too brittle to be useful. Tempering is a process by which the steel is heated to specific temperature well below the hardening temperature and then cooled. The slight heating of the steel relieves some stress and adds toughness to the material. There is a delicate balance,

though, because with toughness comes softness. Care is needed to make sure your part is tough, but will also maintain an edge.

Each tool steel has a different composition and specific heat treatment parameters. Make sure to get a datasheet on whichever tool steel you are using and follow it as closely as possible. Improperly hardened tools can fail, which makes for a dangerous situation.

PART III:
DESIGN

Design is not mysterious. Certainly, all artistic pursuits, including blacksmithing, have an element of creativity that cannot be taught or explained—the design sensibility of the craftsperson, which will always be individual and irreplaceable. But the qualities that those artists incorporate into their work are based on classical design principles that can be measured and learned. By studying these principles, you can ground your art and give it a sense of continuity with the rest of the viewer's visual experience.

None of these principles are intended to be a checklist—plenty of successful pieces of art incorporate only a few principles. Rather, they are a series of considerations you can apply to your work in its design stages, to ensure you have a firm plan before you expend the energy to create it.

DESIGN PRINCIPLES

SYMMETRY, ASYMMETRY, AND BALANCE

Here are the doors and archway of a large project we completed in Pittsburgh. Being in a historic district, one of the early design requirements was symmetry. Throughout the design process, elements were added and removed to create balance.

Below: This is a fire screen made for a private residence. We worked with architect and designer Lauren Sanchez to create a random, asymmetrical pattern resulting in a modern look.

Symmetry means that, if you were to divide your design along an axis, both sides would be mirror images. The human body is roughly symmetrical, and we find symmetrical patterns inherently harmonious, comfortable, and pleasing. In design, symmetry can be used to create a sense of harmony. However, if symmetry is applied with too much rigor, it can make a design feel stagnant. That's when asymmetry can be used.

In adopting asymmetric elements in your design, it's important to keep an eye on balance if your aim is to keep everything unified. You can use historical ratios to ensure balance in asymmetric designs, like the golden ratio, but the most important thing is understand the role that visual weight and balance play in an asymmetrical design.

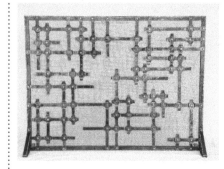

REPETITION

This shows the repeating design elements for a project we completed in downtown Charleston, South Carolina. This pattern repeats throughout the driveway gates, pedestrian door, and balcony guardrail to unify all three separate pieces.

In design, repetition refers to the use of a particular element or theme throughout a piece. Repetition can provide a unifying sense of pattern that makes a design feel complete. It can also make a design seem stagnant and boring if overused.

Within the context of architectural ironwork, most designs cannot help but be repetitive in one way or another. Even just having a repeating stock size throughout a piece is a powerful form of repetition and helps the viewer make sense of a design. Repetitive design can be especially effective when used alongside asymmetrical, chaotic designs to provide contrast.

It can be very time consuming to make many completely unique elements for a design. Designing repetition into a piece can make a strong, budget-conscious statement.

SYMBOLISM

The language of symbolism is a rewarding study, one no artist should ignore—even if you do not choose to use classical symbolism in your work, knowing the allegorical meaning of, say, a pomegranate or a cornucopia can help you avoid sending an undesired message.

Symbols exist within cultural context, which can be very specific to time and place and can be very literal or totally abstract. Take, for example, the daffodil. In the Victorian language of flowers, it represents unrequited love. In *hanakotoba*, the floriography of Japan, the meaning is respect. The daffodil is the national flower of Wales and has been adopted as a symbol of Welsh nationalism. And in the modern United States, it's practically synonymous with spring. That's four different meanings just for one plant.

Even if you are approaching a straightforward design like a fence or a bracket, there is still an opportunity for you to tell a little story or make a statement using symbolism. For customer commissioned work, employing symbolism can be a great way to personalize a piece.

This set of driveway gates by Ambrose Burne explores the idea of using a traditional form (the scroll) in a unique and contemporary way. The smooth, directional curves of the material create an aesthetic of implied movement.

The customer for this project wanted a railing that celebrated her Irish heritage using symbolism. We incorporated giant rhubarb leaves and fuchsia flowers, both iconic Irish fauna, into the design. Harps were also designed into the piece to act as the newel posts.

SCALE, EXAGGERATION, AND IMPLIED MOVEMENT

The eye does not take in any design all at once. It is important for the artist to give the eye a clear path to follow through the design, so the viewer can appreciate every detail. Without a clear path, designs can become muddled and uncomfortable to view, leading to underappreciation, even if all of their elements are high quality. Even if you do not want the viewer's eye to follow a path, understand that directing the eye of the viewer is your responsibility as a designer.

Scale can be an integral component in creating this implied movement, as the eye is naturally drawn to larger masses before smaller ones. A grouping of a few smaller elements (like leaves) around a larger element (like a flower) will give that grouping rhythm and visual interest. Oftentimes, an artist will exaggerate the size of an element in a design. This exaggeration can create a sense of the unexpected—for example, a screen showing a forest of delicate trees surmounted by a large apple upends the viewer's expectations and makes them think anew about the food-producing power of a forest.

But it is not enough to give a variation in scale to the viewer through your design—you also need to provide a roadmap for that viewer to travel. That's where implied movement comes in. Smooth curves and gentle tapers linking decorative elements indicate organic, natural motion, while straight lines and sharp angles are jarring, fast, and abrupt. Curves that build with varying radiuses can indicate fast but smooth motion.

This sculpture is part of a series of pieces based on photographs of particle collisions. The curves are meant to imply explosive motion.

DRAFTING

Here is a typical three-dimensional rendering we might use for a presentation to the customer. This rendering was done by our 3-D designer, Clinton Donellan. Colors and styles are added to the drawing to make it seem more lifelike. The drawing we use for fabrication will be technical, with all dimensions called out.

The name of our company is Robert Thomas Iron Design, and we like to put almost as much emphasis on the design part as the iron part. Of course, we sometimes take on commissions designed by architects, or designers, or even customers with very specific tastes. But whenever possible, we like to control the project from design to installation. The true value we can offer lies in our ability to design as well as forge. As a working blacksmith and designer, I rely on a comprehensive understanding of the material to inform a design. Someone who does not work with forged metal is limited by their lack of knowledge on how

metal moves and what we can achieve when manipulating the material. This is why most outside designs we receive, although beautiful, do a poor job of capitalizing on the forging process.

Even if someone comes to us with a very specific idea of what they want, we almost always push back and try to have at least some influence on the design. Just making a few slight design changes can turn a fabrication project into a forging project. Making small changes like altering the orientation of two intersecting bars can change a welded joint into a riveted joint. Forged

components are what we as blacksmiths can bring to a project that other general fabrication shops cannot. We have a responsibility to our customers to integrate forgework whenever possible because that gives them the most value and allows us to do what we love.

Controlling the design process requires the ability develop and communicate designs effectively. We develop those designs through research, sketching, and drawing in its many forms. We communicate our designs through renderings, 3-D models, shop drawings, and sometimes even maquettes.

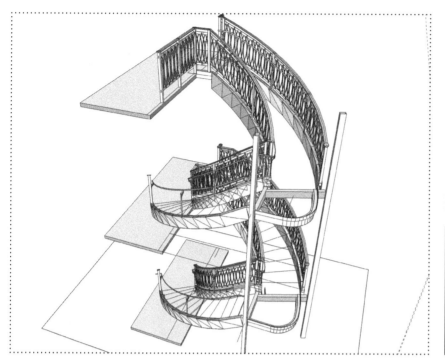

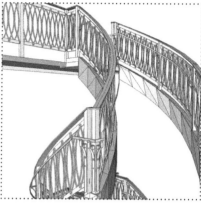

This is a 3-D model Clinton Donellan created for a monumental staircase project we completed in downtown Charleston. More technical than the artistic rendering, the model can be used to understand complex angles and transitions.

For me, the design development process starts with sketching. Even if I already have an idea of what I want in my head, it will need to be resolved on paper before moving forward. Often, I will sketch many quick iterations of a design in a sketchbook before moving forward with one and cleaning it up. This part of the process can either be quick or very involved, depending on the scope of the project. I'm not trying to work out actual construction here, just get a broad idea of design intent and aesthetic. I will often work with my mom, Angela, who is a professional artist and designer, at this point. As a non-blacksmith with a great design sense, she is great at coming up with beautiful design. It is up to me to make it work as a forged piece.

The aesthetic will often be adjusted based on the eventual forging operations involved. Knowing how I intend to put something together allows me to highlight certain structural elements as design elements. This is a style of design reserved for those with a firm understanding of the material and goes back to the idea that being a blacksmith and designer ultimately makes for a better design.

In the case of a commissioned work, the design will have to be approved by the customer in most instances. This means it will have to be rendered in such a way as to clearly communicate the aesthetic and structure of the piece. In the case of two-dimensional work, a clean drawing is usually enough to show intent.

For three-dimensional presentations, we usually create a 3-D model and sometimes even an animated video orbiting around the model to present to the customer. This is not as complicated as it sounds. We work with Clinton Donellan, a very talented 3-D CAD operator, to translate our two-dimensional drawings into three dimensional models. With a 3-D model, every angle and detail can be easily shown to a customer so they totally understand exactly what they're getting.

Most commercial projects will require shop drawings prior to beginning forging. Shop drawings are detailed technical drawings drawn to scale with dimensions called out. They are drawn in the style of architectural drawings and usually in plan (overhead) and elevation (side) views. All of these drawings are easily rendered from a 3-D model using layout software. When it comes time to actually build a project, some shop drawing can even be printed out in full scale on a large plotter.

Ultimately, getting comfortable with design work can only benefit your forging practice. Avoiding design means limiting your work to the designs of others. Embracing design means setting yourself apart and working toward the possibility of true innovation.

PART IV:
PROJECTS

This section follows the RTID team through the many processes involved in making various tools and decorative pieces of ironwork. The projects have been designed to encompass a wide variety of tooling and techniques. For virtually every step of every project, there are multiple potential techniques that can be used to achieve the same end result. Different smiths may use totally different processes or tools to achieve the same result. The steps described in this section are just the way we do it.

These processes are a result of our collective experience and available tooling. I fully expect our processes to continue to evolve as we gain more experience and learn from our peers. Yours should too. For that reason, these projects should be treated as case studies rather than technical instruction. Try it our way and then experiment to figure out which processes work best for you.

TOOLING

SIDE BIT TONGS
FORGED BY MATT GARTON

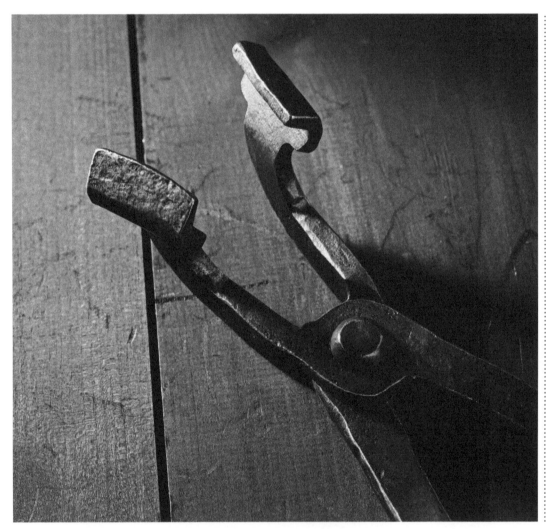

MATERIALS NEEDED

⅝" (16 mm) square bar, 8" (203 mm) long, two pieces

TOOLS USED

Cross peen forging hammer

Ball peen forging hammer

Anvil

Power hammer or striker with sledge

⅜" (10 mm) round punch

Swage black with V-groove

½" (13 mm) ball punch

⅝" (16 mm) Square tongs

Anvil fork

The ability to make your own tongs is an absolute must for any blacksmith. Although there are multitudes of commercially made tongs on the market, we make most of ours in-house. Usually, we find that we need a particular size or style, and forging them is the easiest and quickest option. Since so many tongs are special purpose, it's hard to pick a favorite, but the side bit style tongs Matt makes in this project are extremely versatile and still quite sturdy. A huge advantage for the type of work we do is the ability to grab a long or curved piece of stock in the middle rather than the end.

NOTE: Forge both tongs simultaneously to ensure consistency throughout the process. For each step prior to assembly of the tongs, perform the processes on both tongs before moving on to the next step. Exact measurements aren't as important as consistency between the two tongs.

All operations performed at a bright orange/yellow forging heat unless otherwise noted.

STEP 1: MARKING OUT

Mark each bar 2 inches (51 mm) from the end with a center punch.

STEP 2: ISOLATING THE BIT

Set down 2 inches (51 mm) of the bar to half its thickness (5/16 inch [8 mm]). This isolates the material needed for the bit. Start the set down by tilting the workpiece down a few inches (76 to 101 mm) and hammering directly over the edge of the anvil using half hammer-faced blows on the nearside of the anvil.

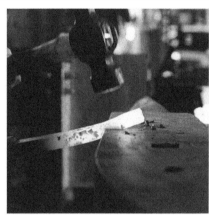

STEP 3: FORGING THE JAWS

Flip the workpiece and move it to the farside edge of the anvil, tilting it up and setting it down about 5/8 inch (16 mm) from the end of the bar. Move back to the nearside edge of the anvil and draw out the isolated material to 2½ inches (64 mm). The section remains 5/8 × 5/16 inch (16 × 8 mm).

STEP 4: FORGING THE HINGE PLATE

To forge the hinge plate, rotate the workpiece one-quarter turn to the left and line up the edge of the first set down with the farside of the anvil while holding at a 45 degree angle to the edge. Then, forge the material down to half the thickness of the bar (5/16 inch [8 mm]). This is a widely used and taught tong-making process throughout the U.K. and U.S.

STEP 5:
FORGING THE REINS
(HANDLES)

In order to isolate the material used for the reins, create another set down on the farside edge of the anvil 1 inch (25 mm) behind the start of the hinge plate. Forge the beginning of the rein to $5/16 \times 1/2$ inch (8 × 13 mm) and leave the rest to be drawn out with the power hammer. The resulting hinge plate is $1 \times 7/8$ inch (25 × 22 mm). Draw out the reins to about 16 inches (406 mm) long with a gradual taper resulting in about a $5/16$ inch (8 mm) square section at the end of the rein.

STEP 6:
SPREADING THE NIBS

Next, spread the end of the nibs to $2 \times 3/4$ inch (51 × 19 mm) using the cross peen hammer. Square all edges and faces using the corner of the anvil, taking care to keep the hinge plate very flat.

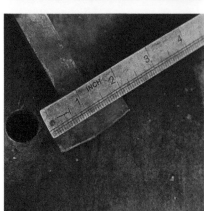

STEP 7:
PUNCHING THE HOLE

Using the ³⁄₈ inch (10 mm) round punch, punch both hinge plates in the center of the plate. Flatten the surface again after punching.

STEP 8:
BENDING THE BITS

Alternating between the horn of the anvil and the anvil fork, bend the bits 90 degrees using a heat isolated on the bend.

STEP 9:
SETTING THE NIBS

The tong nib is set using the V swage of the swage block and a piece of square stock driven with a hand hammer. Have a helper hold the tong in place while you drive in the square bar.

STEP 10: RIVETING TOGETHER

Tweak both sides to make sure they're identical and then hot-rivet the two tongs together using a ³⁄₈ × 1 inch (10 × 25 mm) rivet. Once riveted, quickly open and close the tongs while quenching in water to ensure a tight, but moveable, fit.

ANVIL FORK
FORGED BY ROBERT THOMAS

MATERIALS USED

2" (51 mm) square bar, 3" (76 mm) long, 4140 alloy tool steel

TOOLS USED

Power hammer with flat dies or striker and flatter

Hand forging hammer

Anvil

Butcher top tool

Handled chisel

Tongs for 2" (51 mm) square

Tongs to hold material the size of hardy hole

Angle grinder

File

The anvil fork is one of our most often used hardy tools. We have several different sizes for every anvil, ranging from ⅜ inch (10 mm) spacing up to 1½ inch (38 mm) spacing. We also have forks with varying thicknesses of fork material for light and heavy work. Anvil forks are extremely useful for all sorts of bending and scrolling operations as well and three-dimensional bending. By holding the workpiece perpendicular to the fork, pieces can be bent very easily in a flat, two-dimensional plane. Changing the angle of the workpiece, helical bends and twists can be created. In both cases, material can be bent using a handheld bending wrench or bending dog or using the hand hammer.

STEP 1: BUTCHERING THE SHOULDER

Mark the 2 inch (51 mm) square bar at 1½ inches (38 mm) from the end using a center punch on all four sides. Using the marks as a guide, butcher in ¼ inch (6 mm) on all four sides. This isolates the material that will be used for the shank of the tool and creates a crisp shoulder for the fork section of the tool to rest upon. Shown is a low-profile butchering tool under the power hammer, but this can also be done with a handled butcher tool and a striker.

STEP 2: FORGING THE SHANK

Once the material is isolated, forge the shank down to just over the size of the hardy hole on the power hammer. This hardy hole is 1½ inch (38 mm) square, so the shank is forged to approximately 1⁹⁄₁₆ inch (40 mm). Forge the shank the rest of the way very carefully with a striker and set hammer, constantly checking the fit. Once the shank just barely fits in the hole at red heat, drive it in the rest of the way with sledgehammers. As it cools, it will release. This ensures the tightest possible fit, which is very important for an anvil fork because we'll apply pressure from lots of different angles when the fork is in use.

STEP 3: ISOLATING THE FORK

Start the fork section of the tool by forging the other end of the tool down to a 1 × 2 inch (25 × 51 mm) section about 3 inches (76 mm) long, leaving about a ½ inch (13 mm) thick shoulder around the base of the tool just above the shank.

STEP 4: DRESSING THE SHOULDERS

Refine the shoulder using a ½ inch (13 mm) fuller and sledge. Drive the shoulder material down until the tool is firmly seated on the anvil surface all around.

STEP 5: SPLITTING THE FORK

Split the rectangular mass using a handled chisel and sledge to create the fork shape. Cut the cut about three-quarters of the way using a hot cut chisel and finish the split with increasingly wide fullers. This eliminates the inevitable hot-shut that would form through just splitting with a chisel. The ends of the fork should be open about 90 degrees at this point.

STEP 6: DRESSING THE TINES

After allowing the piece to cool, grind the tines of the fork to have a slight radius and finish the surfaces with a file.

STEP 7: SETTING THE TINES

Reheat the fork to forging temperature and set the tines using a ¾ inch (19 mm) spacer held by a helper.

SLOT PUNCH
FORGED BY ROBERT THOMAS

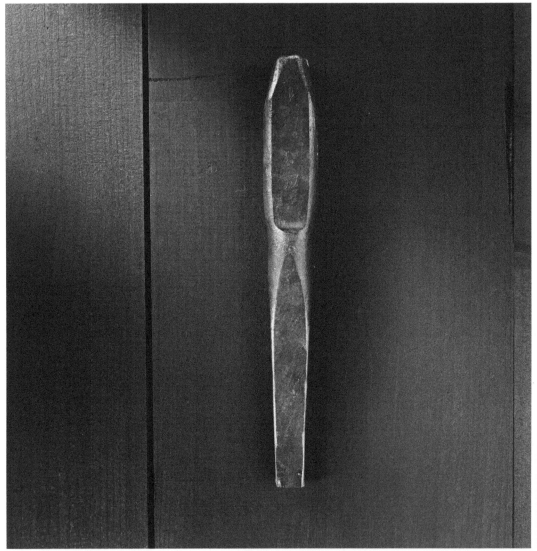

MATERIALS USED

1" (25 mm) round bar, 6" (152 mm) long, tool steel

TOOLS USED

Power hammer with flat dies

Flatter and striker

Hand forging hammer

Anvil

Tongs for 1" (25 mm) round

Belt grinder

The slot punch creates an oval or rectangular hole that usually has the same circumference as the intended finished hole. Because a large amount of material is left around the hole, a beautiful swell forms after drifting. The combination of aesthetics and ease of drifting makes the slot punch our most often used style of punch by far. We have hundreds of different slot punches in different sizes and shapes. Some have wood handles, some are handheld, and some are held with dedicated tongs.

STEP 1: FORGING THE STRIKING END

The striking end of the tool will take a lot of impact through use and upset or mushroom over time. To combat this, forge a short taper on the end of the bar to allow the end to spread out a little before it gets in the way.

STEP 2: FLATTENING THE HANDLE

The top half of the tool gets flattened a little bit on two sides. Take it down to about ¾ inch (19 mm) thick in the flattened section with the other sides left unforged and bulged. This is done to make the direction of the punch easier to feel, especially with a glove.

STEP 3: FORGING THE TAPER

Using the flat dies on the power hammer, start the rectangular taper about ½ inch (13 mm) beyond the flattened handle and forge a parallel taper down to ¾ × ³/₁₆ inch (19 × 5 mm) at the end. Smooth the taper out at the anvil with a striker and flatter.

STEP 4: HEAT-TREATING

Once forging is complete, heat-treat the tool in accordance with the data sheet and dress using the belt grinder.

CHISEL
FORGED BY ROBERT THOMAS

MATERIALS USED

1" (25 mm) round bar, 6" (152 mm) long, tool steel

TOOLS USED

Power hammer with flat dies

Flatter and striker

Hand forging hammer

Anvil

Tongs for 1" (25 mm) round

Belt grinder

A flat chisel is an extremely useful tool that's necessary for many different styles of work. Hot-cutting a bar at the anvil can be a huge time saver as compared to waiting for the bar to cool and using a bandsaw or other means of cold cutting. Some accuracy is lost when hot cutting with a chisel, but many operations don't require a precise cut. We use many different hand-held and handled chisels in our shop, but the straight, simple, hand-held chisel made in this project is one of the most versatile. It works well for cutting, chasing, scoring, veining, and other decorative operations.

STEP 1: FORGING THE STRIKING END

Like the slot punch, the striking end of the tool will take a lot of impact through use and upset or mushroom over time. To combat this, forge a slight, short taper on the end of the bar to allow the end to spread out a little before it gets in the way.

STEP 2: FLATTENING THE HANDLE

The top half of the tool gets flattened a little bit on two sides. Take it down to about ¾ inch (19 mm) thick in the flattened section with the other sides left unforged and bulged. This is done to make the direction of the chisel easier to feel, especially with a glove.

STEP 3: FORGING THE BLADE

Using the flat dies on the power hammer, forge a rectangular section just behind the base of the handle down to ½ × ¾ inch (13 × 19 mm). Then, forge a 2 inch (51 mm) chisel taper on the end of the tool using the flatter and striker. After heat-treating, sharpen the end with the belt grinder.

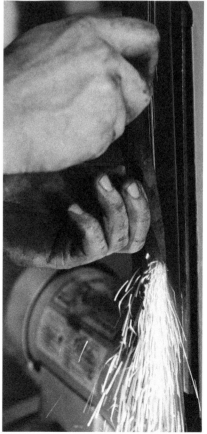

DRIFT
FORGED BY ROBERT THOMAS

MATERIALS USED

1" (25 mm) round bar, 6" (152 mm) long, tool steel

TOOLS USED

Power hammer with flat dies

Flatter and striker

Hand forging hammer

Anvil

Tongs for 1" (25 mm) round

Farrier's rasp

File

Our design style often utilizes swelled holes as a recurring design element. To create a beautiful swell around a hole as part of a pass-through connection or mortise-and-tenon joint, the material around the hole must be driven outward. This is achieved using a drift. There are many different shapes of drifts used for finishing holes, but the one we use most often is a round drift. The round drift is also often used as part of multi-step drifting processes. The 1-inch (2.5 cm) round, hand-held drift created in this project is extremely versatile and can be used for holes from 3/16 of an inch to 1 inch (5 to 25 mm).

STEP 1: FORGING THE STRIKING END

The striking end of the drift is forged down to a slightly smaller diameter than with the slot punch and chisel, about ¾ inch (19 mm). Like the slot punch and chisel, the striking end of the tool will upset or mushroom over time. To combat this, forge a slight, short taper on the end of the bar to allow the end to spread out a little before it gets in the way. In order for the drift to be driven through the hole and release, the striking end must remain smaller than the body of the drift. The striking end of the drift will need to be dressed far more often than that of the punch or chisel to ensure clearance when driving through the workpiece.

STEP 2: FORGING THE TAPER

Using the flat dies on the power hammer, forge a round, parallel taper 6 inches (152 mm) long and ¼ inch (6 mm) in diameter at the end on the opposite end of the bar. Once the taper is rough forged on the hammer, refine it using the flatter on the anvil.

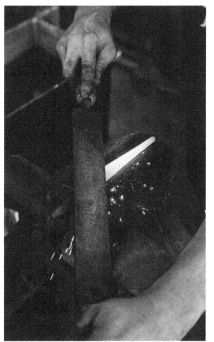

STEP 3: RASPING AND CLEANING UP

Using a helper to hold the workpiece rested in the groove of the vise jaws, clean up the taper and body of the drift with a hot rasp. First, use the coarse side to remove all the high spots and then flip the rasp to the fine side to smooth the surface further. Have the helper slowly rotate the workpiece into the stroke of the rasp during both operations. After heat-treating, finish the surface using a cold file.

HAMMER

FORGED BY ROBERT THOMAS AND MATT GARTON

MATERIALS USED

2¼" (57 mm) round bar, 2½" (64 mm) long, 4140 alloy tool steel

Hickory hammer handle

TOOLS USED

Power hammer with flat dies

Hammer tongs

1" × ⅜" (25 × 10 mm) low profile slot punch

Hand hammer

Anvil

Sledgehammer

Hammer eye drift

1" (25 mm) top and bottom fuller

Quench oil tank

Our shop does not specialize in toolmaking, but we do make most of our hand tools. We don't go to great lengths to make the most beautiful tools we can; we strive to make clean, solid, functional tools that can be put into use quickly. The hammer we make in this project is a typical design for our shop: simple, no-frills, and ready to work.

STEP 1: RESIZING THE MATERIAL

We usually get our tool steel as drop from machine shops, so we end up with all sorts of different stock sizes. This stock started as 2¼ inches (57 mm) round, 2½ inches (64 mm) long. Resize your stock to 1¾ inch (44 mm) square, 3½ inches (89 mm) long.

STEP 2: PUNCHING THE EYE

Using a center punch, mark the piece in the center of the bar's width, but slightly off-center from front to back. Using the slot punch under the flat dies of the power hammer, punch about three-quarters of the way through from one side and then through from the other side.

STEP 3: DRIFTING AND SPREADING

Drift the hammerhead from both sides several times using the swage block as a bolster. After driving the drift, use the fullers on the anvil to spread the cheeks of the hammer, making sure to only forge material on the thicker side of the drift. Repeat this process a few times until you achieve the hole size and spread you are looking for. In this case, we went with medium-sized cheeks for a hammer slightly on the smaller side. For a larger hammer, or if you want to achieve a different size, you may draw the cheeks out more.

STEP 4:
FORGING THE FACE

Forge the face on the smaller end of the bar. Using the flat dies on the power hammer, square up the end of the bar and take down the corners. The resulting face was 1½ inches (38 mm) square. The power hammer dies on our Anyang hammer have about a ⅜ inch (10 mm) radius on one side of the dies. This radius creates a smooth shoulder and a nice transition from the face to the cheeks. Using hammer dies with too sharp of a corner can create a choppy transition, and you may unintentionally fold over the side of your piece, an error known as a hot-shut.

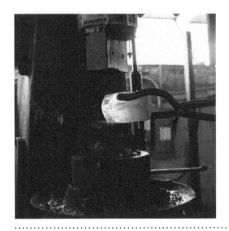

STEP 5:
FORGING THE PEEN

Using flat dies with a radiused edge, carefully forge a short taper on the other end of the bar, starting just behind the eye. After forging it down to about 1 inch (25 mm) at the end, switch to the ¾ inch (19 mm) spring fullers to finish the peen. The end will fish-mouth like it always does. Grind to shape. The resulting peen should be ¾ inch (19 mm) thick with a slight radius on it.

STEP 6:
HEAT TREATMENT AND FINISH

Allow the hammerhead to cool down slowly on the side of the fire before hardening and tempering. Once cool, dress the face and peen with a grinding disc but do not finish-sand them. Harden by quenching the tool in oil at an orange heat. Temper by heating the center of the hammerhead with a hot drift until the faces show a purple color. After the hammerhead is heat-treated, dress the faces with a sanding disc and hang on a burnt hickory handle.

BALL PUNCH
FORGED BY ROBERT THOMAS
AND MATT GARTON

MATERIALS USED

2¼" (57 mm) round bar 2½" (64 mm) long, 4140 alloy tool steel

TOOLS USED

Power hammer with flat dies

¾" (19 mm) spring fuller

Hand forging hammer

1" × ⅜" (25 × 10 mm) slot punch

Hammer tongs

Butcher top tool

Hammer-eye tongs

1" × ¼" (25 × 6 mm) slot punch for power hammer

1½" (38 mm) square tongs

Angle grinder with sanding disc

For the modern blacksmith doing contemporary work, the ball punch has many uses. We use the ball punch most often to spread material around a drilled hole, usually for a rivet. This creates a nice dimple detail that draws more attention to the connection. This technique can be seen in the backplate of the fire tool set project in this book. The ball punch also works very well to isolate material and drive concentrations of material to a different place without affecting material close to the work area.

STEP 1: SIZING THE MATERIAL

Resize the chunk to a 1¾ by 1¾ inch by 3½ inch (44 × 44 × 89 mm) rectangular section and mark for the hole in the center.

STEP 2: PUNCHING THE HOLE

Using the low profile slot punch, punch three-quarters of the way through the piece from one side and then flip the piece over to punch the rest of the way through from the opposite side.

STEP 3: DRIFTING THE EYE

Drift the eye from both sides several times using the swage block as a bolster. Continue to forge the cheeks square after the hole is drifted. Repeat this process several times.

STEP 4: FORGING THE STRIKING END

Forge the striking end of the tool by forging the corners of the end of the bar down to create an octagonal section.

STEP 5: FORGING THE SHANK

Start the ball end of the tool by isolating the mass needed to create the ball. Forge in just behind the eye with the ¾ inch (19 mm) spring fuller. This results in about a 1 inch (25 mm) square fullered section and lump on the end of the tool.

STEP 6: FORGING THE BALL END OF THE TOOL

Forge down the isolated lump to a slight, octagonal taper ending at ¾ inch (19 mm). Cut the shank to the desired length using the hot cut hardy tool.

STEP 7: FINISHING THE TOOL

Heat-treat the ball punch by allowing it to cool slowly on the side of the fire. Once cool, reheat to an orange heat and harden by quenching in oil. Achieve the temper by heating the center with a hot drift until the faces show a purple color. After heat-treating, dress the ball and striking end with the angle grinder and a sanding disc.

FULLER, TOP AND BOTTOM

FORGED BY ROBERT THOMAS AND MATT GARTON

MATERIALS USED

2¼" (57 mm) round bar 2½" (64 mm) long, 2 pieces

TOOLS USED

Power hammer with flat dies

½" (13 mm) spring fuller

Hand forging hammer

Handled flatter

Anvil

Butcher top tool

Hammer-eye tongs

1" × ¼" (25 × 6 mm) slot punch for power hammer

1½" (38 mm) square tongs

Sledgehammers

Swage block

Belt grinder

Fullers are some of the most versatile and often-used tools in our shop. Concentrating the force of a blow into a precise location using a top or bottom fuller allows us to make all sorts of interesting forms. For material isolation in decorative and tool-making applications, a matching set of top and bottom fullers is an indispensable solution. The top and bottom fuller set made in this project can be used independently or as a set, and their uses are only limited by your imagination.

BOTTOM FULLER

STEP 1:
FORGING THE SHANK

Size the rod to 2 × 2 × 3 inches (51 × 51 × 76 mm) square. Mark at 1½ inches (38 mm) from the end using a center punch on all four sides. Using the marks as a guide, butcher in ¼ inch (6 mm) on all four sides. This isolates the material that will be used for the shank of the tool and creates a crisp shoulder for the tool to rest upon. Once the material is isolated, forge the shank on the power hammer down to ¹⁄₁₆ inch (2 mm) over the size of the hardy hole. Forge the shank the rest of the way very carefully with a striker and set hammer, constantly checking the fit. Once the shank just barely fits in the hole at red heat, drive it in the rest of the way with sledgehammers. As it cools, it will release. This ensures the tightest possible fit.

STEP 2:
UPSETTING THE TOOL

Once the shank is sized properly, upset the top of the tool using dual striking to spread out the material to about 2½ inches (64 mm) square. This process also serves to form a very solid and broad shoulder for the tool to rest on. After the upsetting process, square up the chunk of material using a flatter.

STEP 3:
ISOLATING THE FULLER

Isolate the top two thirds of the tool using the ½ inch (13 mm) spring fuller on the power hammer, fullering about ⅜ inch (10 mm) into each side of the tool.

STEP 4:
FORGING THE FULLER

Forge the isolated material down to a thickness of ⅝ × 2½ inches (16 × 64 mm). Use the belt grinder to grind the radius into the face of the tool.

TOP FULLER

STEP 1: PUNCHING THE EYE

Starting with a 1³/₄ × 1³/₄ × 3¹/₂ inch (44 × 44 × 89 mm) rectangular section, punch and drift the eye. Using a center punch, mark the piece in the center of the bar's width, but slightly off-center from front to back. Use the slot punch under the flat dies of the power hammer to punch about three-quarters of the way through from one side and then through from the other side. Drift from both sides several times using the swage block as a bolster until you achieve the hole size and spread desired.

STEP 2: FORGING THE STRIKING END

Forge the striking end into an octagon using the power hammer.

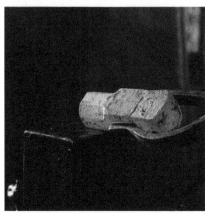

STEP 3: FORGING THE FULLER

Start the fuller end of the tool by pinching off about ³/₄ inch (19 mm) of material using the ¹/₂ inch (13 mm) spring fuller. Forge the isolated mass to match the bottom fuller.

DOUBLE CALIPERS
FORGED BY TYLER BICKERSTAFF

MATERIALS USED

1" × ¼" (25 × 6 mm) flat bar, 14" (356 mm) long

1" × ⅛" (25 × 3 mm) flat bar, 6" (152 mm) long, two pieces

Two ⅜" (10 mm) round washers

One ⅜" × ⅞" (10 × 22 mm)

TOOLS USED

Power hammer with flat dies

Hot chisel—straight

¼" (6 mm) round punch

⅜" (10 mm) round drift

Hand forging hammer

Anvil

Files

Many forging projects require specific material sizes and thicknesses not always found on the rack. In these cases, the first operation of the of the process is resizing the material. A great tool to use to ensure that a forged section is consistently sized is a set of dual blacksmith's calipers. Blacksmith's calipers differ from machinist's calipers in that they have a long handle so they can safely be used to measure hot material during the forging process. They are also generally sturdier and not as precise as a set of machinist's calipers might be. In this project, Tyler makes a set of calipers with a traditional design with a forged and filed finish.

STEP 1: SPLITTING THE BAR

Using the hot chisel, start by splitting 1 inch (25 mm) of the end of the 1 × ¼ inch (25 × 6 mm) flat bar, making the cut right down the middle of the bar. Lock the bar in the vise and cut an additional ¼ inch (6 mm) down into the slit. This starts to spread the two points that will become the inside tips of the calipers.

STEP 2: SHAPING THE POINTS

Forge down the points over the horn of the anvil using a hand hammer, allowing the horn to curve the points into shape.

STEP 3: FORGING THE BODY OF THE TOOL

Using the flat dies on the power hammer, forge a 7 inch (178 mm) long section down to ⅜ × ¼ inch (10 × 6 mm), leaving an untouched section just behind that will become the hinge plate. Leaving about ¾ inch (19 mm) of material untouched, forge the handle of the tool into a long, oval shape 8 inches (203 mm) long.

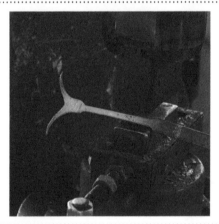

STEP 4: FORGING THE HOOK

Cut off the excess material on the end of the handle leaving 2 inches (51 mm) of untouched material on the end of the handle. Set down 1 inch (25 mm) of that material to form the hook at the end where the tool will be hung. Curve the hook around the horn of the anvil into a 1 inch (25 mm) diameter circle.

STEP 5:
PUNCHING THE HOLE

Punch the hinge plate in the center and drift it open to ⅜ inch (10 mm).

STEP 6:
FORGING THE LEGS

Forge the 1⅛ inch (29 mm) flat bars down into 8 inch (203 mm) tapers ending in sharp points. Curve the legs over the horn of the anvil, making sure to keep them identical and match them to the corresponding points on the body of the tool. Once they are curved, punch and drift the holes to match the tool and cut the excess off using the hot chisel.

STEP 7: FILE SHAPING

File to get smooth surfaces throughout the tool before assembly.

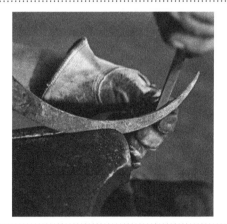

STEP 8: ASSEMBLY

Rivet the calipers together using washers on both sides to help the legs be tight but movable after assembly. Some tweaking may be needed to make everything work properly.

BLACKSMITH'S SQUARE
FORGED BY MATT GARTON

MATERIALS USED

1½" × ⅜" × 16"
(38 × 10 × 406
mm) flat bar

TOOLS USED

Power hammer
with flat dies

¾" (19 mm) round
power hammer
fuller

Hand forging
hammer

Straight chisel

Anvil

Round punch

Set hammer

90 degree backing
plate for vise jaws

The blacksmith's square is a heavy-duty square with a long handle that can be easily rested on a hot workpiece to check for squareness. Many forged parts like tenons, corners, and joinery need to be completely square, and it's much more efficient to be able to check them while they're still hot as opposed to waiting for them to cool down.

STEP 1:
FORGING THE HANDLE

Start by fullering halfway into the edge of the bar 8 inches (203 mm) from the end. This isolates half of the bar so you can draw that out for the handle of the square. Draw the isolated mass down to a ¾ × ⅜ inch (19 × 10 mm) section, forming the handle of the bar.

STEP 2:
SPLITTING THE TOOL

Punch a ⅜ inch (10 mm) round hole 7 inches (178 mm) from the unforged end of the bar in the center of the wide face. Using the punched hole as a starting point, cut the bar down the middle using the straight chisel. The cut forms the legs of the square.

STEP 3:
FORGING THE LEGS

After opening the legs of the square to about 90 degrees, forge them to ⅝ × ⅜ inch (16 × 10 mm). Carefully refine the surfaces to make sure they are smooth and flat.

STEP 4:
FORGING THE CORNER

Using a 90 degree backing plate for the vise, drive the material behind the bent corner back into itself with a set hammer. This helps further refine the corner and create a true 90 degree angle.

STEP 5:
CORRECTING THE LEGS

Refine the legs of the square and correct until the angle is perfect.

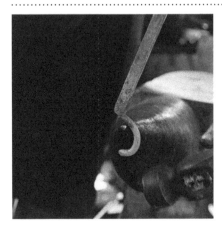

STEP 6:
FORGING THE LOOP

Finally, form a small loop on the end of the handle to allow the tool to be hung up.

TOOL RACK
FORGED BY ROBERT THOMAS AND MATT GARTON

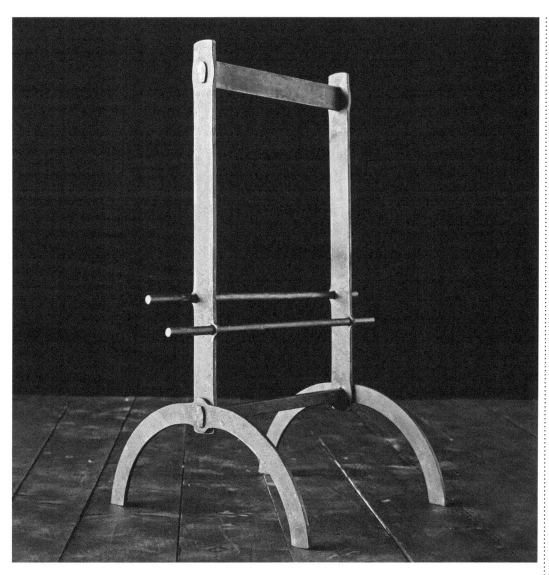

MATERIALS USED

2" × ³⁄₈" (51 × 10 mm) flat bar, 28" (711 mm) long, two pieces

⁵⁄₈" (16 mm) round bar, 24" (610 mm) long, two pieces

2" × ¹⁄₂" (51 × 13 mm) flat bar, 17¹⁄₂" (445 mm) long, two pieces

¹⁄₄" × 1⁷⁄₈" (6 × 48 mm) rivets

TOOLS USED

Power hammer with flat dies

³⁄₁₆" × 1" (5 × 25 mm) slot punch

Butchering tool

Round back flatter

¹⁄₂" (13 mm) slitting chisel

⁵⁄₈" (16 mm) round drift

1" × ³⁄₈" (25 × 10 mm) rectangular drift

Large bending dog

Vertical band saw

Hand forging hammer

Rawhide mallet

Anvil

Custom 10" (254 mm) radius bending jig

Files

Sure, tool organization is great, but hanging your tools in style is essential. In our shop, we have a lot of tool racking on the walls behind the forging area, but we also have several smaller tool racks that can be moved around so that go-to tools are always close at hand.

This tool rack is designed to be versatile and also fun to forge. The design involves several techniques and elements that are useful in many different projects. There are three different hole punching scenarios, heel tenons, straight tenons, and some tricky bending. All of this makes for a challenging build and a beautiful finished product.

UPRIGHTS

STEP 1: PUNCHING THE TOP AND BOTTOM HOLES

The top and bottom holes in the uprights are traditional, punched and drifted parallel rectangular holes. This is a style of hole used widely in traditional joinery. Using the flat dies on the power hammer, punch holes 3 inches (76 mm) from either end of the 2 × ⅜ inch (51 × 10 mm) bar. These will form the corners of the frame. Drift the holes to 1 × ⅜ inch (25 × 10 mm).

STEP 2: SLITTING THE HOLES FOR THE HAMMER RACK RAILS

The holes used to hold the rails for the hammer racking are off-center slit and drifted holes. Off-center drifted holes can be a very cool design feature, but they can also be a little tricky to control.

The holes are placed ¼ inch (6 mm) from the edge of the bar and staggered so the racking bars will accept the hammers hanging at an angle. Drive the tool in from both sides to carefully slit the holes. Once the holes are slit through, follow with a gradual drift, being careful not to drive the tool through the hole after the outside is cool. Since there is more mass on one side of the hole, the material spreads and cools at different rates. If the drift is driven through after the corners of the hole are cold, the outside of the bulge could crack. Perform several cycles of drifting and reheating so the hole is drifted with a controlled bulge that adds interest to the connection and the overall design. Repeat the process on the other three holes.

LEGS

STEP 3: PUNCHING THE HOLES IN THE LEGS

The holes in the legs are a third style of hole, also very interesting and also a little tricky. These holes are the same dimension as the holes in the upright, 1 × ³⁄₈ inch (25 × 10 mm). The difference between the two holes is that these are oriented perpendicular to the bar instead of parallel as the holes in the uprights. In order to make the large material bulge around the holes, start with a parallel slot-punched hole using the same size punch as with the uprights, 1 × ³⁄₁₆ inch (25 × 5 mm). After the initial punch, first drift the hole drifted round, which starts to push the material out. Using a controlled heat right around the area of the hole, upset the bar to turn the hole into an oval shape perpendicular to the direction of the bar. Finish the holes by drifting them to their final dimension using the 1 × ³⁄₈ inch (25 × 10 mm) rectangular drift. The finished result should be a heavily bulged hole that is well worth the extra effort to produce.

STEP 4:
BENDING THE LEGS

To bend the legs, use a quarter circle jig with a 10 inch (254 mm) radius. The jig has a 1 × ⅜ inch (25 × 10 mm) post welded at the top for the hole to mount on and an area around the hole removed to allow for the bulge of material around the hole. Bend the leg around the jig, with the hole sitting on the post at a bright orange heat. Since this is 1½ × ⅜ inch (38 × 10 mm) material, use a large bending dog to apply the force and a rawhide mallet to flatten the bend along the way. After the bend is complete, flip the piece and bend the other leg using the same jig.

CROSSBARS

STEP 5: FORGING THE HEEL TENONS

The bottom crossbar certainly does not need to have heel tenon connections, but they are beautiful and make for a rock-solid joint. The heel tenon is a tenon with an extended shoulder on one side, which adds surface area and stability to the connection. Heel tenons are usually found in the bottom, pivoting corner of a gate frame and are used to prevent sagging under the weight of the gate.

Since heel tenons require a dramatic change in section and are easiest to forge on the end of a longer bar, forge the heel tenon on a bar of larger section and then forge-weld it onto a smaller section to create the bottom frame rail. Make the bottom rail of the tool rack from two separate pieces forge-welded in the center.

During the forging process of the heel tenons, two identical pieces are made, so every operation listed next is done twice.

Start the forging process by upsetting the end of a 1½ × ¾ inch (38 × 19 mm) flat bar that is cut long enough to hold without the use of tongs (about 30 inches [762 mm]). The extra mass also makes it easier to upset into a floor anvil. Upset the end to about 2 inches (51 mm) wide while maintaining the ¾ inch (19 mm) thickness dimension. Once the upset is roughed out on the floor anvil, finish it using a hand hammer at the anvil. During this process, you will also push the material to one side so that three sides of the bar remain parallel and all the material is pushed up to the top. Refine the shape over the horn of the anvil so the resulting bar end is angled toward the curve.

Cut and isolate mass for the tenon using the low-profile butcher tool under the power hammer. Cut the tenon directly into the point at the top of the bar end. Once the shoulders on three sides are cut in and defined, forge the tenon out with a set hammer and striker. This is a careful process where the bar is flipped often to prevent the tenon from being forged too much to one side. The finished dimension of the tenon should be 1 × ⅜ inch (25 × 10 mm) and about 2 inches (51 mm) long. The excess will be cut off prior to assembly.

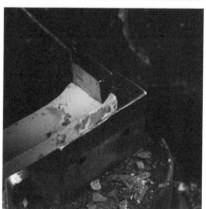

Use the power hammer to draw down the bar behind the heel to 1 × 3/4 inch (25 × 19 mm), 8 inches (203 mm) behind the shoulder of the tenon. Refine the curved section using the half round side of the flatter and refine the straight section using the flat side. Cut the bar off 8 inches (203 mm) from the shoulder of the tenon and scarf the end in preparation for the forge weld.

Now that both parts of the bar are completed, heat them simultaneously to a welding heat with no flux. Be very careful to get the heat just right on both bars. With a helper holding one part, scarf weld the two pieces together and forge the section back to size under the power hammer. With the proper heat preparation and flat, constant pressure of the power hammer, the weld takes completely in a single heat. The weld should be almost undetectable after the bar is forged back to the proper dimension.

Finish the shoulders of the heel tenons with a square file and check with a blacksmith's square. The finished length of the cross bar is 16 inches (406 mm) from shoulder to shoulder.

The upper crossbar is made in a much less glamorous way that the lower. Since the tenons are only shouldered on two sides of the 2 × ³⁄₈" inch (51 × 10 mm) flat bar, they can be laid out with silver pencil and cut with the vertical band saw. These tenons can also be forged, but cutting them yields the same result.

STEP 6: ASSEMBLY

The assembly process is very simple on this piece. Start by hammering over one side of the top crossbar tenon while it's locked in the vise. Hammer the bottom tenon over the same way, except it goes through both the upright and the legs at the bottom. Have a helper support the upright while you hold the legs and hammer over the tenon. Repeat the process on the side of the rack, this time, backing the crossbars on the anvil. Slide the ⁵⁄₈ inch (16 mm) round bars through the off-center holes to form the hammer racking.

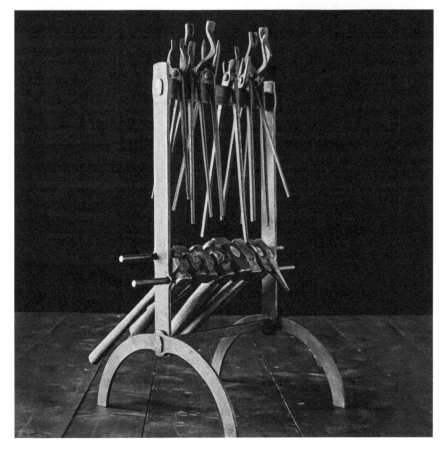

BOOKENDS
FORGED BY JP SHEPARD AND MATT GARTON

MATERIALS USED

1" × 3/16" (25 × 5 mm) flat bar, 26" (660 mm) long, two pieces

3/4" (19 mm) round bar, 1" (25 mm) long, four pieces

2" × 1/2" (51 × 13 mm) flat bar, 17 1/2" (445 mm) long, two pieces

1/4" × 1 7/8" (6 × 48 mm) rivets

TOOLS USED

Power hammer with flat dies

3/4" (19 mm) round power hammer fuller

Drill press

Hand forging hammer

Anvil

Scrolling pliers

Bending forks

A great chef once told me to try to cook dishes without using garlic and olive oil because it would make me a better cook. Although the combination makes everything delicious, it's also ubiquitous. Constantly relying on the garlic and olive oil combination prevents the cook from exploring a multitude of other flavor combinations. Free from the shackles of conventional cooking, true breakthroughs are possible and signature dishes can be born.

The scroll is the garlic and olive oil of contemporary ironwork. The scroll is perhaps the most popular iron design element of all time. Originally used as gussets, iron scrolls have been used by designers and architects for millennia to both tasteful and occasionally excessive ends. The scroll is a ubiquitous symbol for ironwork, but, like the old garlic and olive oil one-two punch, relying on it as a design element can put your creativity on sleep mode.

Unless specifically requested by the client (which is often the case), we rarely design ironwork with scrolls. I have nothing against scrolls and actually really enjoy forging them since they are such a great exercise in fluid forging and forming. When we do design with scrollwork, we often try to incorporate the bevel scroll because of its flowing lines and three dimensionality. It's also a very tricky forging, which keeps the smith engaged and challenged.

These bevel scroll bookends are designed to be a modern take on an old classic. The simple L bracket frame and cylindrical standoffs have an industrial feel in sharp contrast to the delicate bevel scrolls which act as the gussets.

STEP 1: FULLERING AND BENDING THE FRAME PIECES

Mark and fuller the 2 × ½ inch (51 × 13 mm) flat bars 6¾ inches (171 mm) from the end of the bar. Hammer the fuller ¼ inch (6 mm) into the bar and then create a 90 degree bend at the fuller mark.

STEP 2: FORGING THE SCROLLS

Forge a 3 inch (76 mm) taper on the edge of the ³⁄₁₆ inch (5 mm) flat bar and scroll it until it forms a J. Do this in 2 to 3 heats, working back and forth from the face to the horn of the anvil. Once the shape is created, forge a bevel into both edges of the scroll using the rounding side of a farrier-style rounding hammer.

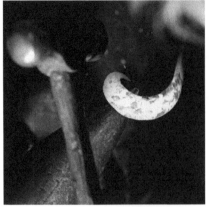

STEP 3: FORMING THE THREE-DIMENSIONAL BENDS

This is the tricky part. Carefully bend the end of the scroll in the opposite plane over the horn of the anvil while gradually twisting the workpiece to create a bend and twist simultaneously. The resulting shape gradually twists 90 degrees while it bends into a scroll shape.

STEP4: FORMING THE REMAINDER OF THE SCROLL

About 6 inches (152 mm) from the end of the bar, complete the 90 degree twist and scroll the rest of the bar parallel to itself using the scrolling tongs and a drawing as a guide.

STEP 5: ASSEMBLY

Line up the scrolls, standoffs, and frames and mark for rivet holes where everything comes in contact. Drill the ³/₄ inch (19 mm) round standoffs in the center and drill corresponding holes in the scrolls and frames. Countersink the holes on the back of the frames so that the rivets can spread and remain flush on that side. Using the horn of the anvil for a bolster, hammer over the rivets to complete assembly.

TRIVET
FORGED BY JP SHEPARD

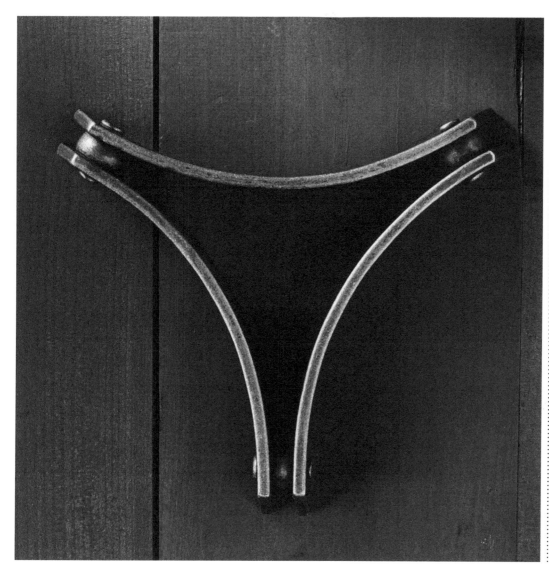

MATERIALS USED

1½" × ¼" (38 × 6 mm) flat bar, 9" (229 mm) long, three pieces

¾" (19 mm) round bar, 1" (25 mm) long, three pieces

¼" × 1⅜" (6 × 35 mm) rivets

TOOLS USED

Power hammer with flat dies

Mitering horizontal band saw

Drill press

Cordless drill

Hand forging hammer

Anvil

Bending jig for 7" (178 mm) radius arc bends

Bending forks

90 degree backing plate for vise jaws

This trivet is a good exercise in geometric symmetry, jig-making, upsetting, and simple assembly. The clean, modern design highlights the rivets and upset spacers as a major design element, making for a beautiful piece with very few components. A similar design becomes a central element in the side table project outlined later in this book.

STEP 1:
BENDING THE ARCS

Cut both ends of the flat bars off at 75 degree angles and heat the bars to an even heat using a propane forge. Bend them around an arc jig using bending forks.

STEP 2:
FORGING THE SPACERS

Upset the ¾ inch (19 mm) round bars to a thickness of ⅝ inch (16 mm) using the power hammer. These will become the spacers between the legs of the trivet.

STEP3:
DRILLING THE HOLES

Mark the bent flat bars in the center of the bar, ½ inch (13 mm) from the end. Using the drill press, drill ¼ inch (6 mm) holes for the rivets. Clamp the spacers in a vise and drill the spacers through the center.

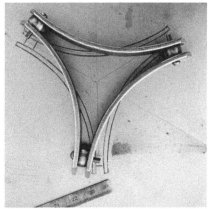

STEP 4: ASSEMBLY

After wire brushing, rivet the parts together using a hand hammer. You want to wire brush the parts *before* final assembly because it's easier to get in tight spots before the parts are together.

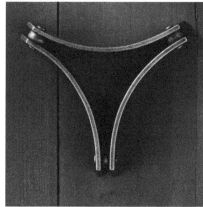

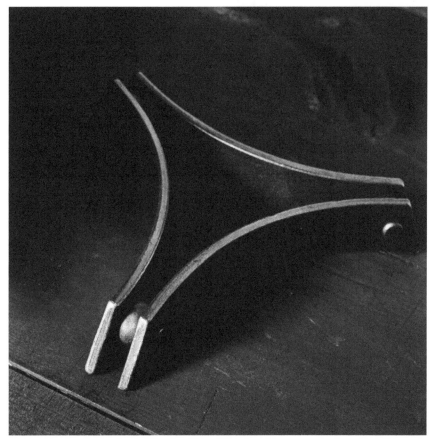

DOOR HANDLE
FORGED BY ROBERT THOMAS

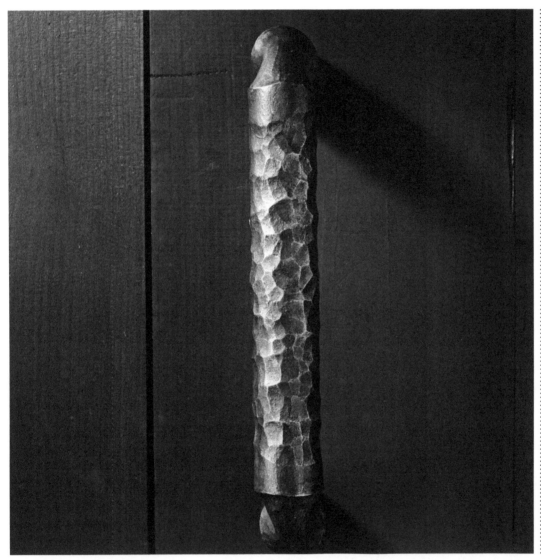

MATERIALS USED

1¼" (32 mm) round bar, 11" (279 mm) long

⅜" × 16 bolts, or M10 × 1.5 bolts, 1½" (38 mm) long

TOOLS USED

Power hammer with fullering dies

¾" (19 mm) spring fullers

Hand forging hammer

Rawhide mallet

Anvil

Drill press

⅜" × 16 tap, or M10 × 1.5 tap

Door hardware has been forged by blacksmiths for millennia. In early years, hardware was likely designed for utility and security. By the time of the Baroque period, door hardware, like most ironwork, was designed for form as well as function. Even during times of limited ornamentation, door handles have always been forged with special design consideration. Maybe this is because they're pieces of ironwork that must be interacted with regularly. Door handles must be designed with both aesthetic and tactile considerations. While most ironwork needs to be designed to be seen, a handle must be designed to be seen and felt.

STEP 1: FULLERING THE CORNERS

Mark the bar 2 inches (51 mm) from each end using a straight chisel to mark several points around the circumference of bar. Using the ¾ inch (19 mm) fuller, fuller the bar down to ¾ inch (19 mm) diameter on both marks. This stretches the bar approximately 1½ inches (38 mm) total.

STEP 2: TEXTURING

Texture the handle itself using fullering dies by lightly hammering the bar in a random pattern at several different angles. The texture works best at a red heat using many light blows.

STEP 3: BENDING

Bend the ends of the bar over 90 degrees using a rawhide mallet to avoid marring the piece since so much force is required to make the tight bend. Once cooled, drill and tap the ends in the center for the mounting hardware.

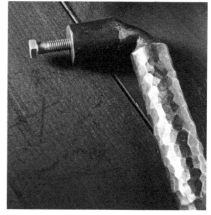

FIREPLACE TOOL SET
FORGED BY ROBERT THOMAS, MATT GARTON, AND JP SHEPARD

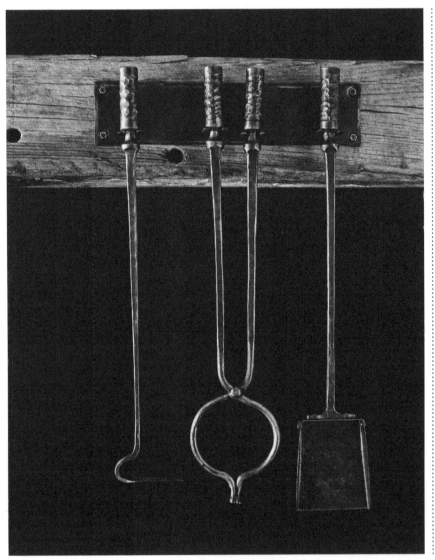

MATERIALS USED

1¼" (32 mm) round bar, 8" (203 mm) long, 2 pieces

1¼" (32 mm) round bar, 10" (254 mm) long, 2 pieces

¼" × 1" (6 × 25 mm) flat bar, 2½" (64 mm) long

³⁄₁₆" × 4" × 16" (5 × 102 × 406 mm) plate

6" × 5" (152 × 127) 16 gauge (1.5 mm) plate

⅜" × 1½" 10 × 38 mm) rivets

¼" × 1" (6 × 25 mm) rivets

³⁄₁₆" × ⅜" (5 × 10 mm) rivets

TOOLS USED

Power hammer with fullering dies

¾" (19 mm) spring fullers

Hand forging hammer

Ball punch

Straight chisel

½" (13 mm) slitting chisel

⅜" (10 mm) round drift

Anvil fork

Rawhide mallet

Anvil

Drill press

The fireplace tool set, or companion set as it's sometimes called, is another very common project for past and present smiths. An iron fire tool set is an essential part of any hearth setup and is a staple of most blacksmiths' product lines. Many smiths have their own signature styles and designs. There are three main factors that can affect the success of a fire tool set design: function, aesthetics, and ergonomics. First and foremost, these are tools and should be designed with that in mind. The user will, presumably, be using the tools every time they light a fire and will have to retire them if they don't do the job. Using the same handle as the door handle project, the tools in this project work very well from an ergonomic standpoint. The handles are substantial and heavy, which balances the weight of the other end of the tool. When making your own tool set, you may often find that a beautiful design does not always function or feel good in the hand. It can be helpful to make a single prototype tool and test it before making an entire set.

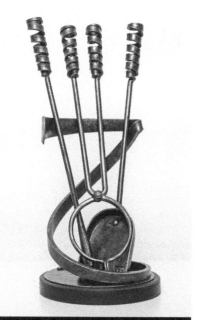

James Price made this wrap fire tool set. This set seeks to move away from the conventional hanging arrangement seen in most companion sets. A fluid ribbon of steel encircles the three tools which in turn sit on a slate base. The handles on the tools echo the form of the base.

STEP 1: LAYOUT DRAWING

Create a full-scale drawing. This gives you a reference point to work toward when forging. Here, all three tools and the mounting plate with hooks are illustrated.

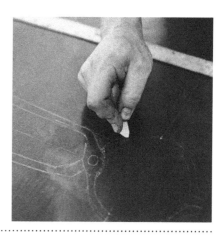

STEP 2: FORGING THE HANDLES

Forge out all the tool handles at the same time to ensure consistency. Mark all four pieces of 1¼ inch (32 mm) round at 4 inches (102 mm) and fuller to ¾ inch (19 mm) round using the ¾ inch (19 mm) spring fuller. Texture the handle using fullering dies by lightly hammering the bar in a random pattern at several different angles. The texture works best at a red heat using many light blows.

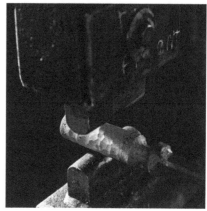

STEP 3: ISOLATING THE SHAFTS

Just behind the fullered section, fuller the bar again using the ¾ inch (19 mm) spring fuller. This time, forge the section down to ⅝ inch (16 mm) square, leaving a 3½ inch (89 mm) length isolated on the end of the bar for the two 8 inch (203 mm) pieces and 5½ inches (140 mm) left for the 10 inch (254 mm) pieces.

STEP 4: FORGING THE SHAFTS

Forge the isolated material down in gradual tapers to form the shafts of the tools. The taper lengths are as follows:
- Rake: 26 inches (660 mm) terminating at ⅜ inch (10 mm) square.
- Tong reins: 27 inches (686 mm)— the last 15 inches (381 mm) forged to ½ inch (13 mm) round.
- Shovel: 20 inches (508 mm) terminating at ½ inch (13 mm) square.

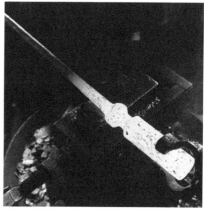

FIRE RAKE

STEP 5: FORGING THE RAKE

Using a cross peen hammer, forge the end of the fire rake by forging a slight taper on the end of the bar and spreading the last 4 inches (102 mm) into a wedge shape about 2 inches (51 mm) wide at the base with a blunt tip. Forge the edges flat to make it easier to scrape the floor of the fire box for cleanup. Forge the flat wedge slightly concave using the cross peen driven into the V die of the swage block. This bend creates strength and rigidity for the blade of the rake. After the rake end is formed, bend it to shape using the anvil fork.

TONGS

STEP 6: FORGING THE TONG REINS

For the tong reins, slit and drift ⅜ inch (10 mm) holes 12 inches (305 mm) from the end of the bars using a slitting punch followed by a ⅜ inch (10 mm) round drift.

STEP 7: FORGING THE TONG NIBS

Drive a ball punch into the end of the tong nib to spread that material and isolate the nib.

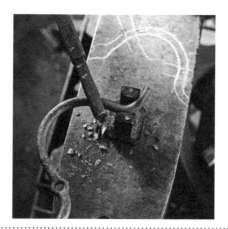

STEP 8: BENDING THE TONG JAWS

Bend the jaws of the tongs into a semi-circle shape to match each other and bend the reins just behind the hole.

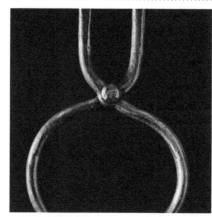

STEP 9: RIVETING THE TONGS

Rivet the two tongs together and tweak them to make them work properly.

SHOVEL

STEP 10: FORMING THE SHOVELHEAD

Form the shovelhead by bending the edges of the 16-gauge plate up and riveting the sides together forming a shovel shape.

STEP 11: ATTACHING THE SHOVELHEAD

Split the last 1¹⁄₂ inches (38 mm) of the taper on the end of the shovel handle using the straight chisel. Once cut and cleaned up, punch each resulting end with the ball punch and drill it through for riveting. Rivet the handle to the shovelhead with two ¹⁄₄ inch (6 mm) rivets.

WALL MOUNTING PLATE

STEP 12: TEXTURING THE PLATE

Texture the 3/16 inch (5 mm) wall mounting plate and make impressions for the mounting screws with the ball punch.

STEP 13: FORGING THE HOOKS

Make the hooks by splitting 1/4 inch (6 mm) flat bar and forging it down into a fork shape sized properly to grab the fire tools securely around the fullered section. Forge the shank of the hook by forging the flat bar down to 1/2 inch (13 mm) round material, ball punching, and drilling the end.

STEP 14: ATTACHING THE HOOKS

Rivet each hook onto the backplate and bend to the proper angle for hanging using the torch and scrolling pliers.

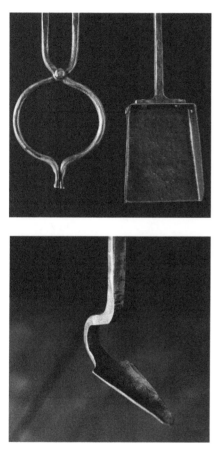
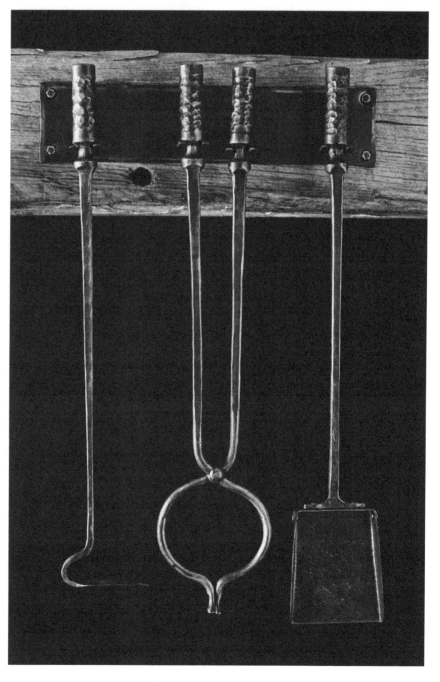

BOTTLE OPENER
FORGED BY ROBERT THOMAS

MATERIALS USED

1" (25 mm) round bar, 4½" (114 mm) long

TOOLS USED

2" (51 mm) fuller

Power hammer or striker with sledge

Hand forging hammer

¾" × ⅛" (19 × 3 mm) slot punch

1" (25 mm) round drift

½" (13 mm) ball punch

1" (25 mm) tongs

The bottle opener is something that every blacksmith will forge in their career. Most smiths end up making quite a few. Because a bottle opener is a popular forged product, it can be challenging to create one that stands out. After making many different sizes and styles, I can attest that there are two attributes that cannot be compromised in bottle opener design.

1. Function: The bottle opener must be able to easily open a bottle cap. If the opener does not function fluidly, it simply will not work and might cause the bottle to break.

2. Ergonomics: The bottle opener has to fit and be comfortable in the hand. If it doesn't feel right, it will become a pretty paperweight.

After these two stipulations have been satisfied, the design can be as creative as possible.

The design in this project works well in the hand and does its job.

Bowline bottle opener by J. Powers Shepard

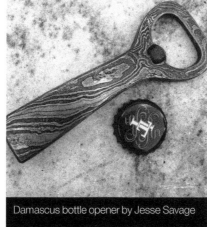
Damascus bottle opener by Jesse Savage

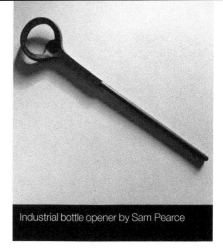
Industrial bottle opener by Sam Pearce

STEP 1:
UPSETTING THE BAR

Heat the entire bar up to a bright yellow color and quench approximately 1 inch (25 mm) of one end and 2 inches (51 mm) of the other end of the bar, resulting in a yellow off-center heat with black, quenched ends. Working quickly to avoid the material overcooling in the center, upset the bar until the center bulges out to about 1½ inches (38 mm). This will almost always cause the bar to jog and lean over to one side. Do not try to correct this; it will work to your advantage in the next step.

STEP 2: FULLERING

Heat the entire bar to a bright yellow heat and grasp the shorter end of the bar with the tongs. Place the bar horizontally on the anvil with the slumped side down and drive the round fuller into the crease between the upset and non-upset sections of the bar. Rotate the bar 90 degrees and alternate fullering to drive the material to the center. The resulting piece should stretch back out to 5½ inches (140 mm).

STEP 3: PUNCHING AND DRIFTING

First, flatten the drawn out end of the bar so that you have a nice even flat surface to punch through. Next, center the slot punch on the end of the bar, leaving ½ inch (13 mm) of material past the end of the punch. With the bulging side down and hanging off the back of the anvil, drive the punch through the workpiece until you feel it bottom out. Flip the piece over and, punch through, driving out the slug. Take another bright yellow heat and, alternating directions, open the hole to 1 inch (25 mm) round using the 1 inch (25 mm) drift. Refine the shape using the horn of the anvil and a hand hammer. This will open the hole up to approximately 1¼ inches (32 mm).

STEP 4: CREATING THE LIP

Drive the ½ inch (13 mm) ball punch into the bottom edge of the punched hole to produce the lip that will grab the edge of the bottle cap to pry it off. At this point, the opener end of the piece should have naturally bent slightly upward. If it has not, bend the opener upward by tapping it with a hammer over the edge of the anvil. Test the opener on a bottle to make sure it works and refine the curve if necessary.

SIDE TABLE

FORGED BY ROBERT THOMAS AND JP SHEPARD

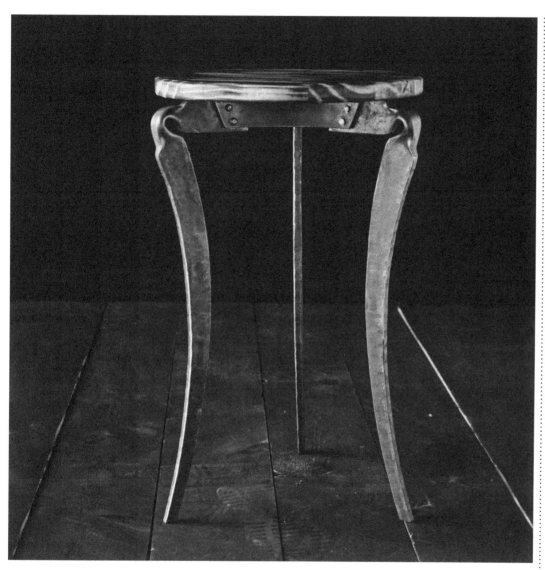

MATERIALS USED

2" × ½" (51 × 13 mm) flat bar, 24" (610 mm) long, 3 pieces

1½" × ¼" (38 × 6 mm) flat bar, 9" (229 mm) long, 3 pieces

Six ¼" × 1½" (6 × 38 mm) rivets

TOOLS USED

Hand forging hammer

Power hammer with flat dies

3" (76 mm) fullering die saddle for the power hammer

Fly press with three point bending tooling

Flatter

7" (178 mm) radius arc bending jig

Bending wrenches

2" (51 mm) flat bar tongs

Center punch

Silver Pencil

Drill press with ¼" (6 mm) bit

Its size and versatility make a side table a great starter project for furniture production. It's also much easier to manage as a solo project than other pieces of furniture. This modern side table base is designed to have a contemporary aesthetic, which works well with a simple, round wood or glass top. The design incorporates many of the techniques described in the book, such as project layout, controlled tapering, fullering, and riveting.

STEP 1: FORGING THE LEG TAPER

Forge a 22 inch (559 mm) taper on the ends of the 2 inch (51 mm) flat bars that will become the table legs, maintaining the ½ inch (13 mm) material thickness as you forge down the taper. The taper is flat and constant and terminates at a width of ¾ inch (19 mm). After forging the taper, there is 6 inches (152 mm) of unforged material left. The tapers are left rough after initial forging and smoothed with a flatter. Use the flatter to refine the surfaces of the taper and make sure all three legs are identical.

STEP 2: FULLERING THE LEG CORNER

Place a center punch mark 5½ inches (140 mm) from the unforged end of the bar. The mark needs to be deep because it must be visible when the material is yellow-hot. Using the 3 inch (76 mm) fullering die on the bottom die of the hammer, fuller the bar down to a thickness of ½ inch (13 mm), taking great care to make sure the workpiece and tool are aligned properly. This step must be achieved in one heat to ensure the material spreads consistently, so it is important the material is a bright yellow heat and each strike is hit with full force. The resulting shape is forged partly by the fullering die, but also by the flat die above.

STEP 3: BENDING THE LEGS

Using the fly press, start the bend on the thicker end of the bar using the residual heat from the fullering operation. The thick side of the bar is carefully bent to match the drawing for the first 6 to 8 inches (152 to 203 mm) of the bend. Only bend this much hot because the rest of the arc can be bent faster cold. Bend all three legs to match and then allow to cool slowly without quenching. Once cool, finish the arcs using the fly press.

STEP 4: BENDING THE CORNER

Heat the fullered corner of the leg back up to an orange heat and bend the leg to match the angle of the layout drawing. Use bending posts that are bolted to a steel table for this bend. After the leg is bent, both ends will be slightly longer than the length they are drawn in the layout. These get trimmed later.

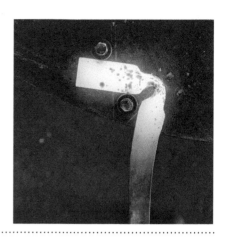

STEP 5: FORGING THE CURVED CONNECTING BRACKETS

Cut and bend the curved brackets that connect the legs at the top of the table by bending them around an arc jig using bending forks. Once bent, drill two ¼ inch (6 mm) holes ¾ inch (19 mm) from the end of the bars and parallel with the cut edge.

STEP 6: ASSEMBLY

Cut the tops of the legs at the same angle as the connecting brackets, 4 inches (102 mm) from the edge of the fuller on the bottom edge of the bar. Line up the tops of the legs so that 1¼ inches (32 mm) is sandwiched in between the connecting brackets. Transfer punch and drill the holes in preparation for riveting. Once all the parts are drilled, test fit everything and bolt together with ¼ inch (6 mm) bolts. When everything is lined up properly, switch the bolts for rivets one by one until the whole thing is riveted together.

Carefully level the table and mark the feet for cutting. Cut the legs off evenly to make the table stand at 30 inches (762 mm) tall with a 1 inch (25 mm) wood top.

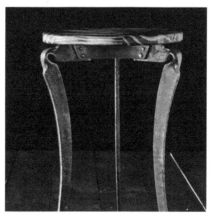

CASE STUDY

GARDEN GATE

DESIGNED BY JOHN WINER. FORGED BY JOHN WINER, ROBERT THOMAS, TYLER BICKERSTAFF, MATT GARTON, AND JP SHEPARD

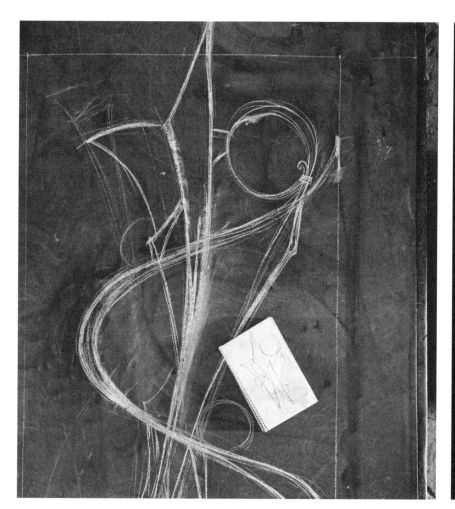

This is John Winer's original concept drawing in small and full scale.

The outer rectangle represents the actual aperture we needed to fill. The practical function of the gate would be to create a barrier that fills that space. The design would go through several more iterations before we started forging.

As a professional musician and blacksmith, many of John's designs are musically driven. The intent with this design was to play with the idea of blacksmiths working in harmony, like musicians. The central theme of the design is a an abstract figure playing a harp and music going out in all directions. Although the layout changed a some since this design iteration, the harp-player theme remained in the finished piece.

As artist blacksmiths, our designs come from many places. Some very specific design briefs come directly from the client or an architect. Sometimes, the client has no idea what they want and is open to ideas. Sometimes, we are forging portfolio pieces and have no design constraints whatsoever. Scenarios where we have zero control or total control over the design process both present their own challenges. Even in the cases where the client has no idea what they want, we are still constrained by a multitude of factors affecting whether or not a design will work in a given space, such as surrounding architectural style, functionality, and budget, to name a few. Each project presents its own specific set of challenges, and we must have a ready supply of design ideas to solve problems and make our work unique.

In our shop, the best fuel for the design engine is process. Through the actual process of forging a particular piece or shape, we often stumble on a new way to solve a design problem. Sometimes, these revelations come in the form of mistakes that end up in the scrap bin until a project comes along that requires that specific design solution. Although this happens very often when working on our own projects within the shop, the effect is magnified when working with other artists collaboratively.

The following project is a case study in the power of craft collaboration. In this project, our team collaborated with John Winer to create a sculptural garden gate from design to execution. Each person involved lends their own perspective and working style to create a piece much greater than the sum of its parts.

In a loosely constrained collaborative project like this, the design is constantly evolving. The original gate design came from the mind of John Winer, but as we worked and started to create the complex shapes, we allowed the design to morph and change based on how the parts were turning out. Since the parts were very sculptural and were being made by five different blacksmiths, they all came out just a little different. None of us could simply forge John's vision the way he would; we could only forge our own interpretation of his vision. Of course, on a more simple, traditional design, there would be far less open to interpretation, and we could count on everyone to produce the same products.

John forged the central element out of 6 × ½ inch (152 × 13 mm) plate using the aggressive drawing dies for the 100 kg Beche hammer to rough out the shapes. Here, he is forging the point on the top end of the bar.

Working the lower end of the bar, John draws out a drastic taper with a huge, fishtail end. He uses the drastic taper to draw the viewer's eye directionally up the bar.

John continues to drastically taper the center of the bar that will serve as the structural and visual center of the gate. I work in the background on a long taper for another element.

When multiple people work together forging a project, there's a great energy and excitement. Scenes like this one are a great example of the harmony John was trying to capture in the gate design. A lot can be accomplished in a short window of time when everyone is enthusiastic.

JP holds the workpiece while John upsets the bottom edge of the bar. Wanting to leave as few straight lines as possible, John curves and shapes every surface of the bar.

After the taper is forged, the bar is curved using the cone mandrel for backing. Forging the piece over the cone mandrel at a specific angle produces a smooth, consistent curve. John makes use of the cone mandrel throughout the project for all the smooth curves we had to create. I learned a great deal about cone mandrel technique in working with John on these pieces.

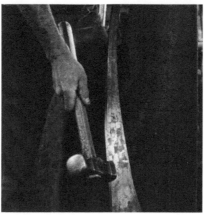

I work on bending a circular element using the vise and a bending wrench.

Everyone is working in harmony on different elements of the gate.

John checks the drawing and we discuss the addition of more elements to fill empty spaces in the design. We decide that the design should fill out the space more for security purposes being that it is a gate.

John and JP use the Smith and Striker technique to forge down a bar and add texture. Working with a striker gives the process still more harmony where blacksmiths can feed off of one another's energy.

Matt and Tyler fan out material using a handled fuller and sledge. They are careful to make a smooth spread and also leave even texture.

Matt isolates material for the element that will become the handle of the gate. The roundback flatter is great for this kind of work.

The fly press is great for controlled, three-point bending. I'm using a light touch to bend a piece of forged silicon bronze.

In a very clever alternative to forging a large, sharp corner, John and JP chisel cut tapers and open them up to form the same shape. Once the cuts are open, they use a series of fullers and flatters to refine the surfaces and finish the curve. The ends of the bar are then drawn down using the power hammer.

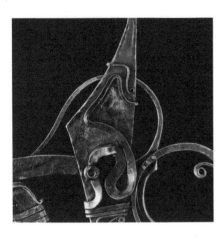

Joinery methods become just as much a part of the design as the bold, flowing lines and implied movement of the main elements. In sharp contrast to the swooping curves, we opt to use busy, tightly wound wraps to make our connections. John winds the central wrap in a whimsical, free-form design that serves as point of interest as well as a structural feature. The wrapped connection is something that can cheapen a design if executed poorly, or, as it has in this case, add to design if done well. John Winer's wraps are a signature aspect of his design style and he has developed them into interesting and unique methods of joinery. We also use a few interesting riveted joints and tension connections throughout the piece to add interest wherever two elements join together.

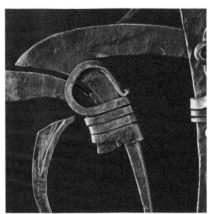

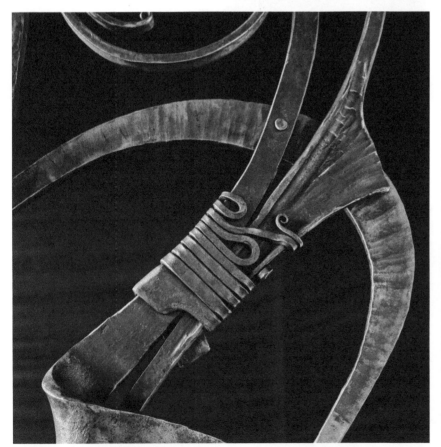

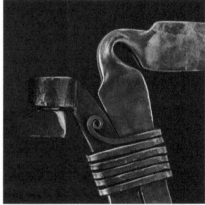

Opposite: The finished gate differs significantly from the original design. This is okay because this project was more like an experiment than a commission. This project was about exploration and pushing the limits of our understanding of forged metal. I believe the finished project was success, but even more successful was our collective development as craftspeople through the act of collaboration.

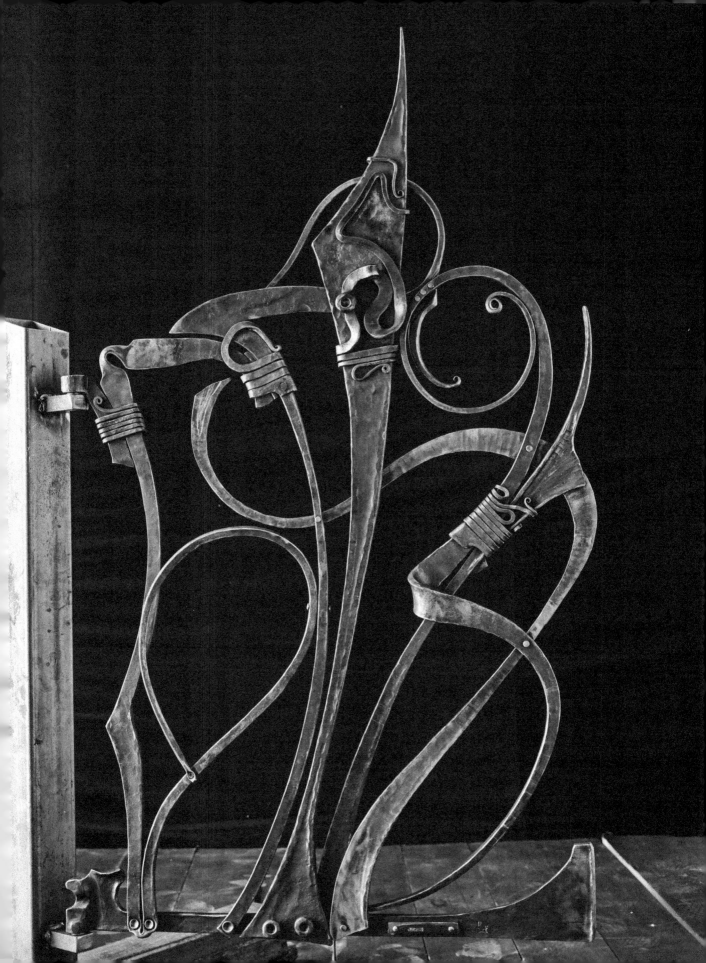

ACKNOWLEDGMENTS

Much of my career, including the writing of this book, would not have been possible without the love and support of my beautiful wife, Natalie. No matter how crazy things get or what time-consuming projects come my way, you never tell me I can't do something. You always find a way to support me and help pick up the slack when I'm overwhelmed. With you by my side, I feel like I can do anything. Thank you.

To my daughter, Rhett, thank you. You were only two months old when I started writing this book so you probably don't remember how much you helped me, but you did. When I was tired from forging all day and didn't want to sit down and write, you gave me a reason to keep working. When the stress of running a business and writing a book at the same time started to get to me, playing with you and watching you laugh would bring me back. When all I needed was a good night's sleep, you let me get it—sometimes.

To my sister, Sarah, thank you for teaching me to appreciate the craft of writing. Thank you for helping organize my jumbled mind and get it down on paper. Thank you for the hours of research, proofreading, revisions, and critique you provided at a moment's notice. Thank you for making mundane facts about metal sound exciting. Thank you for teaching me how to use a semicolon. Without having you as a sister, I would not have taken on this project, and without your help, it would have not been a reality.

Thank you to Sully Sullivan. Thank you for your time and your vision. Your photographs make our craft look better than I ever thought it could. Thank you for getting as excited about this project as I was and approaching it with the same enthusiasm. Thank you for taking such great photos that the book would have been incredible without a single word of text.

A huge thank you to the RTID team: Matt, Tyler, and JP. Thank you for all the long nights and hard work preparing for this project. Thanks for holding down the fort while I was writing. Thanks for continuing to make incredible ironwork. Without you guys, there is no way I would have been able to pull this off!

Thank you to John Winer for coming and working with us and sharing your knowledge, techniques, and perspective on the craft. Thank you for helping make the projects in this book a reality. Thank you for reminding us how important it is to have fun while we forge.

Thank you to everyone who ever taught me something about blacksmithing. Thank you to Adrian Legge for teaching me how to make my first pair of tongs and for teaching me how to execute complex architectural designs. Thank you for helping me with the content of this book through your thoughtful, blunt, and downright harsh critiques.

Thank you Kheir Aker for teaching me that the language of blacksmithing is universal and that it can be the bridge between countries, cultures, and religions. Thank you for showing what a burning passion for the craft looks like.

And finally, thank you to everyone who contributed images of their work to this project: John Winer, Patrick Quinn, Andrew Chambers, Ambrose Burne, James Price, Sam Pearce, Jesse Savage, and Steve Howell.

ABOUT THE AUTHOR

Robert Thomas began tinkering with a hammer and anvil in his first garage shop in 2009. He then attended Hereford College of Arts in England, where he worked with master smiths in the artistic blacksmithing degree program. He has studied metalwork with renowned artists in England, France, Sweden, Czech Republic, Ukraine, Israel, and accross the United States.

Robert and his team have won several awards in blacksmithing and design, including:

2012: 1st place, Iron Work Exhibition; Ivano-Frankivsk Blacksmith Festival, Ukraine

2012: 1st place, Team Forging Competition; Ivano-Frankivsk Blacksmith Festival, Ukraine

2012: 2nd place, Tri-County Show; Malvern, England

2012: Featured demonstrating team member, World Blacksmith Forum; Helfštýn, Czech Republic

2016: Silver medal, gates and doors; NOMMA Top Job Competition

In 2013, Robert moved to Charleston, South Carolina, and founded Robert Thomas Iron Design, quickly gaining a reputation for designing and forging fine architectural and sculptural forgework. Today, RTID creates unique and complex ironwork projects for clients throughout the country.

Robert lives just outside of downtown Charleston with his wife and spends most of his time playing with his daughter Rhett, and Izzy, his goldador pup.

INDEX

www.ingramcontent.com/pod-product-compliance
Ingram Content Group UK Ltd.
Pitfield, Milton Keynes, MK11 3LW, UK
UKHW051023270325
456714UK00004B/31

9 781631 593819